Castles of Ireland

Castles of Ireland

BRIAN DE BREFFNY

Photographs by

GEORGE MOTT

With 151 illustrations, 15 in colour,
plans and a map

THAMES AND HUDSON

For Ulli
who 'lived in castles and lived in shacks'

Title page: Dromore, Co. Limerick

Filmset and printed in Great Britain by
BAS Printers Limited, Wallop, Hampshire

Contents

List of castles illustrated

ASHFORD *Co. Mayo*
ASKEATON *Co. Limerick*
AUGHNANURE *Co. Galway*
BALLINGARRY *Co. Limerick*
BALLINLOUGH *Co. Westmeath*
BALLINTOBER *Co. Roscommon*
BALLYLEE *Co. Galway*
BALLYNACARRIGA *Co. Cork*
BALLYSAGGARTMORE *Co. Waterford*
BELFAST *Co. Antrim*
BIRR *Co. Offaly*
BLACKROCK *Co. Cork*
BLARNEY *Co. Cork*
BRITTAS *Co. Tipperary*
BUNRATTY *Co. Clare*
BURNCOURT *Co. Tipperary*
CAHIR *Co. Tipperary*
CARRICKFERGUS *Co. Antrim*
CARRICKKILDAVNET *Co. Mayo*
CARRICK-ON-SUIR *Co. Tipperary*
CARRIGAFOYLE *Co. Kerry*
CASTLE BALFOUR *Co. Fermanagh*
CASTLE BERNARD *Co. Cork*
CASTLE CARRA *Co. Mayo*
CASTLE GARDE *Co. Limerick*
CASTLE MATRIX *Co. Limerick*
CASTLE OLIVER *Co. Limerick*
CHARLEVILLE FOREST *Co. Offaly*
CLONMINES *Co. Wexford*
CLONONY *Co. Offaly*
COOLHULL *Co. Wexford*
CREAGH *Co. Galway*

DOE *Co. Donegal*
DONEGAL *Co. Donegal*
DROMORE *Co. Limerick*
DUBLIN *Co. Dublin*
DUN AENGUS *Inishmore*
DUNAMASE *Co. Leix*
DUNDRUM *Co. Down*
DUNGORY *Co. Galway*
DUNLUCE *Co. Antrim*
DUNSANY *Co. Meath*
DUNSOGHLY *Co. Dublin*
ENNISKILLEN *Co. Fermanagh*
GLENARM *Co. Antrim*
GLENSTAL *Co. Limerick*
GLENVEAGH *Co. Donegal*
GLIN *Co. Limerick*
GLINSK *Co. Galway*
GOSFORD *Co. Armagh*
GRANAGH *Co. Kilkenny*
GREEN CASTLE *Co. Down*
GRIANAN OF AILECH *Co. Donegal*
GURTEEN-LE-POER *Co. Waterford*
HILLSBOROUGH *Co. Down*
HOWTH *Co. Dublin*
HUMEWOOD *Co. Wicklow*
JOHNSTOWN *Co. Wexford*
KANTURK *Co. Cork*
KILCASH *Co. Tipperary*
KILCOLMAN *Co. Cork*
KILKENNY *Co. Kilkenny*
KILLEEN *Co. Meath*
KILLUA *Co. Westmeath*

KILLYLEAGH *Co. Down*
KILLYMOON *Co. Tyrone*
KINSALE (Charles Fort) *Co. Cork*
KNOCKELLY *Co. Tipperary*
KYLEMORE *Co. Galway*
LEAMANEH *Co. Clare*
LEAP *Co. Offaly*
LEIXLIP *Co. Kildare*
LIMERICK *Co. Limerick*
LISMORE *Co. Waterford*
LOUGH CUTRA *Co. Galway*
LUTTRELLSTOWN *Co. Dublin*
MALAHIDE *Co. Dublin*
MALLOW *Co. Cork*
MAYNOOTH *Co. Kildare*
MONEA *Co. Fermanagh*
MONKSTOWN *Co. Dublin*
NARROW WATER *Co. Down*
NENAGH *Co. Tipperary*
NEWTOWN *Co. Clare*
PARKE'S CASTLE *Co. Leitrim*
PORTUMNA *Co. Galway*
RATHMACKNEE *Co. Wexford*
ROCKFLEET *Co. Mayo*
ROCKSTOWN *Co. Limerick*
ROODSTOWN *Co. Louth*
ROSCOMMON *Co. Roscommon*
ROSSCLOGHER *Co. Leitrim*
SLANE *Co. Meath*
THOMASTOWN *Co. Tipperary*
TRIM *Co. Meath*
TULLIRA *Co. Galway*

Foreword

The Shorter Oxford English Dictionary defines a castle as: 'a large building or set of buildings fortified for defence; a fortress. Retained as a name for large mansions which were formerly feudal castles.' In our personal selection of buildings in Ireland we have included castles built for defence, castles built to look as if they were built for defence, and even those toy-castles that just have a 'castle' look, dependent mainly on their castellation. Our choice was made from among a great number of castles which dot the country. County Limerick alone once boasted over four hundred medieval castles, Cork over three hundred, Tipperary, Galway and Clare each between two and three hundred, and Kilkenny nearly two hundred.

The castles we have chosen have met a variety of fates. Some are cared-for National Monuments, some are uncared-for National Monuments. Several are still private residences, some opulently furnished. Their inhabitants include a duke, a marquess, two earls, a count, two barons, a baronet, a knight, a business man and a farmer. Some are abandoned ruins. At Bunratty Castle tourists sip mead and savour syllabub to the strumming of harps at twice-nightly medieval-style banquets between transatlantic flights. Carrickfergus Castle is a museum, Dublin houses the offices of Government. Ashford is a sumptuous hotel, Ballingarry a cowhouse. A ewe was suckling her lambs in Clonmines 'Town Hall'. Two castles, Glenstal and Kylemore, have become Benedictine Abbeys, and house schools. Gosford and Johnstown are Agricultural Institutes. Leap Castle houses a persistent ghost. This variety of fates is representative, but the queerest destiny of all has surely been reserved for Tandragee Castle, Co. Armagh, which we have not included: this ducal extravaganza is now a potato crisps factory.

Locations of castles illustrated

Introduction

It may well be argued that the castle was introduced into Ireland by the Anglo-Norman knights in the years following their invasion of Ireland in 1170. The Irish Rulers, however, despite their ignorance of the advanced military techniques of the Normans, had built fortresses for some centuries before the invasion. These were intended as impregnable rather then defensible seats, providing a place where the chief and his retainers could enjoy a measure of protection from human and animal marauders and their cattle could be driven into the safety of an enclosure.

The earliest of these *duns* are the hill-forts of the Iron Age, which began in Ireland about 500 BC. A whole hill-top, sometimes an area of several acres, was enclosed within a dry-stone wall or cashel and a protective ditch was dug on the inside or the outside of the wall. The inhabitants of that period were nomadic in their habits, and archaeological evidence suggests that the hill-forts were not consistently inhabited, nor occupied for long periods of time. It has been suggested that they served as places of assembly and as cult centres. It is true that some of the hill-forts were constructed on the site of Bronze Age necropoli, and that these may have continued to attract interest under the pre-Christian priest-kings. There are the vestiges of a typical hill-fort in Co. Kildare; this is Dun Aillinne, which may have been a seat of the Kings of Leinster. Here the ditch is outside the wall, enclosing an area of about twenty acres. In places the wall was as much as fifteen feet high. There was also a hill-fort on the more famous hill of Tara, a royal and religious site in prehistoric times which became the official seat of the High-Kings of Ireland, retaining its importance under the Christian High-Kings until the eleventh century. There a hill-fort was constructed in the Iron Age on the 'Mound of the Hostages', a burial place of about 1800 BC. It consists of a bank with a ditch outside it, enclosing an area in which later two ring-forts were built.

The ring-fort was a more defensible fortification than the hill-fort because it enclosed a much smaller area. It is unusual to find ring-forts built inside hill-forts, like the ones at Tara; they were usually situated on level ground. A wall of mud or stones with a ditch outside it was built to enclose a small area in which huts of mud, rushes or timber could be erected. This ancient arrangement of a small cluster of homesteads sheltered and protected by a wall and ditch survived in Ireland at least into the seventeenth century; it appears to have become obsolete only with the end of the Gaelic order and the Plantations. The little ring-forts with earthen walls were usually no more than practical residential compounds, but larger ring-forts with stone walls and underground passages were also built. These were certainly eminently defensible buildings, and treasure could be stored in cavities or chambers constructed in the thickness of the walls. An example of a simple ring-fort, just 150 feet in diameter, can be seen at Danestown, Co. Meath. A typical small fort at Cahermacnaghten in Co. Clare continued in use until the seventeenth century. There are vestiges of a two-storey medieval gate-house built to guard the entrance. The O'Davorens had their famous law school in the fort in the Middle Ages and into the seventeenth century. It was there that Brehon laws were expounded. As late as 1675, when the fort was described as 'O'Davoren's town', it was still inhabited; a sizeable house and domestic offices stood within the walls of the enclosure which measured about one hundred feet in diameter.

The most impressive example of a ring-fort with stone walls, however, is the magnificent Dun Aengus on Inishmore in the Aran Islands. Built on the edge of a cliff towering two hundred feet over the fierce Atlantic breakers, it has triple landward defences formed of three rows of almost concentric semi-circles. The innermost defence has chambers in the thickness of the walls and wall-walks. Entrance to the enclosure is by a flat-headed tunnel-passage. Outside the fort proper thousands of lethal-looking stone stakes called *cheveux-de-frise* are placed to discourage intruders. Beyond them again is another protective wall. Another imposing ring-fort, the Grianan of Ailech, is among the castles illustrated later in the book (p. 134).

Another type of defensive dwelling constructed in the Iron Age and continuing in use until after the Middle Ages was the promontory-fort, built on a spur jutting out into the sea or a lake. Often a ditch was dug on the landward side across the neck of the peninsula to provide further protection. The best example in Ireland, as difficult of access today as when it was built, is Dunbeg fort on the Dingle Peninsula of Co. Kerry. This was built on a steep-sided promontory jutting out into the Atlantic and protected on the landward side by four defensive banks of stone and earth. It is a National Monument, but a visit to it is described in the Guide as 'very dangerous'.

Dun Aengus, Inishmore, Aran Islands

The fort of Caherconree, also in the Dingle Peninsula, may be classed with the promontory-forts although it is surrounded not by water but by lower-lying land. It is one of the places associated with the adventures of CúChulainn whose beloved, Blathnad, was snatched and married and carried off to the fort by CúRoi; the faithful Blathnad connived at her abductor's defeat and assassination by CúChulainn.

The *crannóg* or lake-dwelling was also an invention of the Iron Age, and was closely related in concept to the promontory-fort. Built of mud, timber, or stone as the occasion and its importance demanded, the *crannóg* was a fort on an islet, often an artificial one, built up in a lake or on a marshy shore, and accessible only by boat, or by tortuous secret paths through the marsh or under water. The castle of Rossclogher (p. 192) was built on an early *crannóg*.

It seems that the concept of using a castle as a tool to achieve military supremacy, to defend the home territory or hold a conquered one, reached Ireland from abroad several decades before the arrival of the Anglo-Norman and Cambro-Norman mercenaries in 1170. The 1120s and 1130s were years when new ideas in building methods and design filtered to Ireland from the Continent. According to the *Annals of Loch Cé*, Tirlogh O'Conor, King of Connaught, erected a castle (*caislean*) at Athlone in 1129. The purpose of this building was to provide a base for his incursions eastwards into Meath. The *Annals of Clonmacnoise* record that only two years later this castle at Athlone was burned by a thunderbolt. We are left with no clue to the size or appearance of this castle, but the implication is strong that it was a wooden structure. The first mention of a *caislean* in the Annals is in 1124, when two were erected, both in Connaught. At Ballinasloe in Co. Galway a *caislean* was built in 1124 and accidentally burnt ('burned by casual fire') in 1131. The *caislean* built at Galway in 1124 survived only a year longer than the one at Ballinasloe, being destroyed by a fire in 1132. Again we may infer that these were wooden buildings. Other mentions of a *caislean* occur in the Annals up to 1166 at Collooney, Co. Sligo, and Tuam, Co. Galway, and two outside Connaught, at Ferns, Co. Wexford, a seat of the Leinster kings, and Cuilentragh, Co. Leix.

It is most likely that these twelfth-century castles were fortifications of the same type as those used by the Normans in their conquest of Ireland in the 1170s and elsewhere. Earlier in the century many Irish had travelled in England and France, and it would not be surprising if the King of Connaught and other rulers should have adopted fortifications whose usefulness was proved by the Normans' success in warfare. The Bayeux tapestry includes scenes of the Normans building a fortification. This is basically a flat-topped mound of earth and stones, called a 'motte'. On the top of the motte a timber tower was usually constructed, surrounded with a palisade. At the foot of the motte a crescent-shaped, D-shaped, or U-shaped area called the 'bailey' was also enclosed with palisades and surrounded with a ditch. The useful encircling ditch was easily created when earth was dug out to build up the motte. Only unskilled labour was required to construct the motte-and-bailey castle save for the carpentry of the tower. William the Conqueror's castle built in sixteen days after his landing in England in 1066 would have been such a one as this.

The Anglo-Normans constructed many motte-and-bailey castles in Ireland in the last decades of the twelfth century. Naturally the timber constructions have perished, but mottes can still be seen in various parts of the country, with the outline of the baileys. One of the most impressive mottes in Ireland is at Knockgraffon in Co. Tipperary, built in 1192 as an outpost for an attack on Thomond. The motte at Granard in Co. Longford, where the outline of the bailey protected by a ditch and bank can be clearly discerned, is said to be the highest in the country.

At first the Irish had no answer to this innovation in the arts of war. Even if the known pre-invasion castles were of this type, they were very few and far between, and none of them survived long. Nevertheless, the Anglo-Normans soon realized the necessity of building more permanent and more defensible fortresses if they were to hold their positions in Ireland and expand their control. The newcomers had superior weapons and military techniques, but the Irish had superiority in numbers and were both fierce and reckless in warfare. The King of Connaught, for example, plunged into Meath and forced the foreigners to abandon their fortification at Trim in 1173, only one year after it was built.

At first a simple, strong, stone-built tower, the keep or *donjon*, with the additional protection of a strong surrounding curtain wall, was found to meet the requirements of defence. Wherever possible the castle was built on a natural eminence commanding a wide view of the approaches, or on a site with natural defences like a promontory. The castle of Dunamase is an excellent example (p. 102); its hill-top site had attracted attention for many centuries before. Another example is Castleroche in Co. Louth, where the de Verdons deliberately chose to build their castle up on a remote rocky outcrop rather than at their *caput baroniae* of Castletown on the coastal plain near Dundalk. Carrickfergus Castle in Co. Antrim (p. 65) is one of the best preserved edifices of the first phase of Anglo-Norman building in Ireland. It is a rectangular keep within a curtain wall, built on a low rocky promontory on Belfast Lough.

The Anglo-Normans brought with them to Ireland a developed feudal social system. The King's powerful vassals the barons had under them a corps of knights, whose service they assured to the sovereign, under their command, when needed. In a hostile country, as Britain had been to them on arrival from Normandy, and as Ireland was to them when they arrived from England and Wales, the barons, and eventually also their knights, required a fortified residence which could serve both as a dwelling and as a stronghold from which they could control the area of the country allotted to them.

The rectangular keeps first introduced the novel idea of accommodation arranged vertically in layers instead of all on one level. The ground floor was used for storage and, one suspects, for livestock. For safety, the entrance to the rest of the building was on the first floor, and was reached by a timber ladder which could be withdrawn in times of danger. Usually the apartment on the first floor, the hall, was the principal one. Guards and retainers slept in this hall at night. The knight or constable and his lady had a chamber higher up. The chapel was also installed on an upper storey.

Huts could be erected in the area enclosed by the curtain wall, known in Ireland as the 'bawn'. Sometimes these domestic buildings were stone-built,

(*Opposite*)
An example of the rectangular keep of the late twelfth and early thirteenth century (Carrickfergus)

but the scarcity of surviving foundations and vestiges suggests that more often they were constructed of timber or mud. A description of Swords Castle, Co. Dublin, in the *Liber Niger* in 1326 gives us an idea of the various one- and two-storey buildings which might be found in a sizeable bawn:

There is in this place a hall, and a chamber adjoining the said hall, the walls of which are of stone, crenelated after the manner of a castle, and covered with shingles. Further, there is a kitchen, together with a larder, the walls of which are of stone, roofed with shingles, and there is in the same place a chapel, the walls of which are of stone roofed with shingles. Also there was in the same place a chamber or apartment for the constable by the gate, and four chambers for soldiers and warders, roofed with shingles, under which are a stable and bake-house. Also there were here a house for a dairy, and a workshop which are now prostrate; also there is on the premises in the haggard a shed made of planks and thatched with straw; also a granary, built with timber and roofed with boards; also a byre, for the housing of farm horses and bullocks.

The castle at Swords was built about 1200 as an episcopal manor; the buildings in the bawn mentioned in the description have almost entirely vanished, though the walls of the pentagonal bawn have survived, as well as the strong gateway.

The entrance was the weakest part of any castle and the necessity of fortifying and protecting it was soon recognized. One answer was to build flanking towers from which bowmen could shoot arrows at oncomers from the slits while stones were hurled down on them from the roof of the tower. The entrance could also be strengthened by fitting a portcullis, an expensive and cumbersome but effective device. It consisted of a heavy wooden grill, shod, bolted and strapped with iron, which could be raised and lowered from above through a slot. Grooves for it to run in were cut in the stone at the sides of the aperture. The machinery for raising and lowering the portcullis, a windlass, had to be accommodated above the slot, i.e. over the entrance. This could most easily be achieved by building a room between the flankers and accessible through one of them. This chamber was also put to domestic use, despite the obstruction offered by the windlass, and by the machinery of a drawbridge.

Ditches, or as they are more usually called when filled with water and surrounding a castle, moats, had long been used as a defence. A drawbridge over a moat was a great convenience, providing access in peaceful times but able to be speedily withdrawn in case of attack, obliging the attackers to negotiate the moat while under fire from the towers and walls of the castle. The earliest and simplest type of drawbridge was a plank which was pulled in or pushed out on rollers. A technical advance was the hinged platform which could be raised by pulling in the chains attached to the outer corners. These chains passed through slots above the entrance and were operated by a windlass in the chamber above.

Important castles often further protected their entrance by a building constructed in front of it, called the 'barbican'. The drawbridge could be placed either in front of the barbican or within its walls where it spanned the moat as at Trim (p. 202). An enemy trying to force an entry had then to negotiate not only the portcullis but the narrow passage through the barbican to the

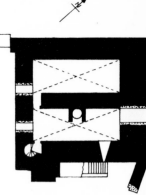

Ground floor

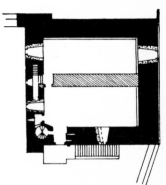

First floor

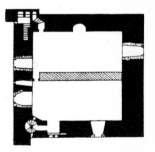

Second floor

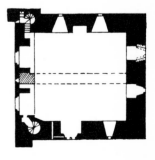

Third floor

Basement

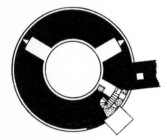

First floor

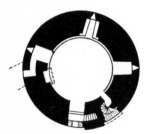

Second floor

Third floor

An example of the
thirteenth-century
cylindrical keep (Nenagh)

door. The upper storey of the barbican which housed the machinery might also have openings piercing the vaulted roof of the passage – 'murder-holes' through which rocks or scalding water could be thrown down on unwelcome persons passing beneath. Murder-holes were a much-liked and useful device and are often to be found in castle passages, though they are sometimes confused by observers with latrine chutes.

As the military architects discovered the vulnerable parts of their castles they set about finding methods of protecting them. Flanking towers were built not only beside the entrance but also at strategic points on the curtain wall, usually at the angles. Already by the end of the twelfth century it was appreciated that angles were vulnerable, and not just the angles of the curtain wall, but the angles of the rectangular flanking towers as well. Corners could be destroyed by picking, knocking out the quoins, or sapping. Before the days of gunpowder the technique used to bring down a wall was first to prop it with wooden planks and then to dig under the foundations to make a hole; a fire of brushwood was laid and ignited in this hole, so that when the props burned through the unsupported wall collapsed. By using this technique on the corner of a rectangular tower it was possible to demolish half the tower and breach the enclosure. For this reason castle-builders began to favour drum-shapes both for keeps and flanking towers. From rectangular or polygonal towers like the keep at Shanid, Co. Limerick, built on a motte early in the thirteenth century, the fashion veered to circular towers like the great keeps of Nenagh, Co. Tipperary (XIV, p. 183), and Dundrum, Co. Down (IV, p. 104), and the cylindrical flankers of Granagh Castle, Co. Kilkenny (p. 126). Frequently, too, the flankers were D-shaped, with the rounded part projecting, like those of Roscommon Castle (p. 194).

Roscommon was a royal castle. The King needed fortresses in strategic positions throughout his Irish dominions, protecting important mountain passes, river crossings, and ports. The maintenance and garrisoning of these royal castles was entrusted to a constable who was appointed and paid by the King, and who received subsidies for building-repairs when they were deemed necessary. It also became imperative for the Government to ensure that the cities which they held were efficiently fortified by walls and a good castle. Dublin was walled between 1204 and 1221 and the walls were fortified with flanking turrets. By the middle of the thirteenth century not only had the major cities like Dublin and Limerick been provided with impressive castles but also smaller important towns like Drogheda possessed satisfactory fortifications. The massive, imposing gateway now called St Laurence's Gate in Drogheda was originally the twin-towered thirteenth-century barbican protecting the entrance through the town walls.

The royal castles were usually built without a keep, the plan being based instead on a powerful curtain wall with towers surrounding a roughly rectangular enclosure. Limerick, Dublin and Roscommon Castles all followed this plan, as does the city-castle of Kilkenny although it was not a royal one.

Ballintober Castle in Co. Roscommon, built about 1300, is the only surviving early medieval castle of an Irish ruler (p. 42). It was the chief seat of the O'Conors of Connaught, who seem long to have been in the vanguard of experimental castle-building and aware of new trends from abroad. It is nearly square in plan with immense polygonal towers at the corners. Obviously it was inspired by the royal castles, and particularly by Roscommon Castle only ten miles distant, which Hugh O'Conor, King of Connaught, had captured in 1276 and held for about four years, time enough to appreciate and study its advantages and amenities.

A castle-plan peculiar to Ireland in the thirteenth century is to be seen at Carlow where one side of the castle survives, and at Lea Castle, Co. Leix, and Ferns Castle, Co. Wexford. This plan has a rectangular keep strengthened at the corners by communicating three-quarter round towers, an arrangement which obviated the vulnerable corners while at the same time retaining the rectangular shape which was infinitely more convenient for residential apartments, whether halls or bedchambers. The circular buildings were so inconvenient, in fact, that some castles, like Green Castle, Co. Down, were still built with rectangular keeps even after their military disadvantages had become evident (p. 126). At Carlow the keep was a perfect rectangle with massive walls nine feet thick and four towers at the corners with walls of the same thickness. Ferns Castle was larger than Carlow, its towers having twice the diameter. Lea Castle was also larger than Carlow. Enniscorthy Castle, Co. Wexford, which was rebuilt in the sixteenth century and restored in the nineteenth, appears to have been on the same plan when it was originally built in the thirteenth century, either by the Prendergasts or by Maurice Rochford who married the Prendergast heiress and inherited the castle on her father's death in 1251. This style is also to be seen at Dunmoe Castle, Co. Meath, of which only two sides survive, but this building has been attributed to the fifteenth century. The castle appears intact in Grose's illustration from a drawing made early in the 1790s. The rectangular castle-plan with circular corner towers was indeed used until a late date. This is known from such examples as Kilbolane Castle, Co. Cork, thought to have been built in the fifteenth or even in the sixteenth century, and the Castle of the Curlews at Ballinafad, Co. Sligo, built about 1590.

Some of the defensive devices used in the castle-building allowed for stylistic decorative developments, especially the machicolation and battlements. Battlements with their crenellations have become the hall-mark of the castle. They are the parapet walls rising above the roof which gave shelter to bowmen or other defenders. Such thin parapets were notched at intervals for practical purposes, thus creating an indented skyline called a crenellation. Behind them was the wall-walk, an uncovered passage along the top of the wall, its width being the thickness of the wall less that of the parapet. Sometimes the wall-walk was widened by making a flooring of planks which jutted out beyond the thickness of the wall internally, supported on that side by stone corbels. On some castle walls rows of such corbels survive although the timber wall-walk they supported has perished. The machicolation was a development of this overhanging surface which came into use by the fourteenth century. Projecting externally from the wall-face, on lintels or arches which stood on corbels, the stone machicolation provided a row of openings through which missiles could be dropped on intruders who were attempting to enter or to undermine the walls. Commoner is the single element of this sort, the machicoulis, which was generally placed over a doorway or

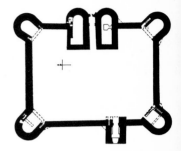

An example of a keepless royal castle with D-shaped turrets (Roscommon before sixteenth-century alterations)

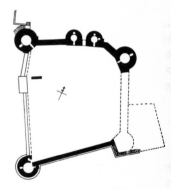

An example of a keepless city castle (Limerick, showing also seventeenth-century alterations)

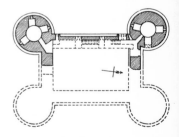

An example of a rectangular keep with cylindrical corner flankers (Carlow, principal floor, dotted lines indicating presumed original walls)

Rockstown, Co. Limerick, one among the four hundred or so tower-houses that dotted the county at the time of the Desmond palatinate.

First-floor plan of a fifteenth-century tower-house (Roodstown)

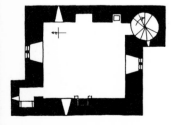

vulnerable angle. Machicoulis built round the angles of rectangular towers and curtain walls, often semi-circular in form, are usually called bartizans.

In the fifteenth century a picturesque form of crenellation called the 'stepped-battlement' is found. Good examples of these battlements may be observed at Coolhull Castle in Co. Wexford (p. 89), at Rathmacknee Castle in the same county (p. 190), and at Blarney Castle in Co. Cork, built about 1446 (p. 54), where they crown a continuous machicolation borne on tall tapering corbels. The origin of these stepped-battlements and parapets has been widely discussed but not satisfactorily solved. They were also used on ecclesiastical buildings such as the cathedral of Kildare at the same period. They are found, too, on buildings in the extreme south-west of France near the present frontier of Spain and across the border in Catalonia. Dr Harold Leask has suggested that the style was brought to Ireland early in the fifteenth century by Irish builders or patrons who had visited the shrine of St James at Compostela, then a popular place of pilgrimage.

There was a lull in both church and castle building during the fourteenth century. First the Bruce invasion of 1315, then the Black Death which reached Ireland in the middle of the century, took a tremendous toll, depleting the country of both finances and craftsmen. By the beginning of the fifteenth century, when Ireland began to recover, the English authorities were occupied elsewhere, first by the Border Wars, then by the French Wars, then by the Wars of the Roses. It is not surprising, therefore, that during this century the English supremacy in Ireland declined and the autonomy of the Hiberno-Norman lords and the Gaelic Irish rulers grew. This shift of power was accompanied by a revival of building activity.

Small medieval towns, like Clonmines in Co. Wexford (p. 86), Carlingford in Co. Louth, or Ardglass in Co. Down flourished. Within their walls castellated town tower-houses were built. Kilmallock, Co. Limerick, fortified by the Earls of Desmond in 1375, was a town of four- and five-storey elegant castles, decorated not only with stone-carving but also with gilding.

The Crown, alarmed by the frequent incursions by the Irish into the Pale, endeavoured to encourage the loyal English residents to build castles by offering them a subsidy. This offer, first made to the gentlemen of Co. Louth in 1429, was extended in the following years to those of the other counties in the Pale. The Statute of Henry VI stated explicitly:

It is agreed that every liege-man of our Lord the King of the said counties who chooses to build a castle or tower sufficiently embattled or fortified within the next ten years to wit twenty feet in length sixteen feet in width and forty feet in height or more, that the Commons of the said countries shall pay to the said person to build the said castle or tower ten pounds by way of subsidy.

A simple three-storey tower which survives at Donore, Co. Meath, was built to these measurements. It has a projecting turret at its south-west corner containing the stair. Roodstown Castle in Co. Louth (p. 192), four storeys in height and with two projecting turrets at diagonally opposite corners, one for the stair and the other containing the garde-robe and some small chambers, was also built in the first half of the fifteenth century, and appears to be another of the many towers whose erection was stimulated by the bounty offered in 1429. It appears that too many liege-men of Meath took advantage of the offer; in 1449 a limit was put on the number of castles built in that county.

Elsewhere in the country, even without the encouragement of the subsidy, towers were built in considerable numbers and all in much the same style, throughout the fifteenth and sixteenth centuries and even into the seventeenth century. The popularity of the tower-house is not at all difficult to explain. It provided on three or, more frequently, four or five storeys, the requisite accommodation for a gentleman and his family. The residential apartments could be placed in safety on an upper or top floor. Until the advent of heavy cannon the tower-house could be defended by just a few warders with an adequate supply of ammunition. When the storehouse on the ground floor was properly stocked and the livestock gathered into the bawn, the inhabitants had the wherewithal to withstand a reasonably long siege. These tower-houses are to be found dotted all over the island. Some were abandoned and have slipped into anonymity. Of many, like Rockstown, Co. Limerick, little history is known. Many became the residences of the English adventurers and settlers who came at the end of the sixteenth and throughout the seventeenth century, and continued, often with lean-to extensions, to serve these families well, into the eighteenth and even the nineteenth century. Kilbline Castle in Co. Kilkenny has an uninterrupted history as a habitation up to a few years ago, and its rooms are still in use as store-rooms for the adjoining farmhouse. At Castle Garde in Co. Limerick (p. 74), the tower-house is still inhabited since its apartments communicate with the residence adjoining it, built in the last century. In many places the tower-houses, like the ancient keeps, have been incorporated into later buildings and have vanished, or all but vanished. In the barony of Kiltartan in Co. Galway the numerous tower-houses gained a new lease of life at the turn of the century when they appealed to the nostalgic tastes of Lady Gregory's coterie. Edward Martyn lived in one, Oliver St John Gogarty bought another, and W. B. Yeats's attachment to Ballylee Castle (p. 44) is well known.

The limited accommodation of the towers was augmented in many places by a detached hall built in the castle enclosure. This was usually a two-storey building with the banqueting-room or audience-chamber above. Examples survive at Askeaton Castle in Co. Limerick (p. 34), built over vaulted foundations in the fifteenth century, and at Adare and Newcastle West in the same county.

Even with the addition of a hall, the rectangular tower and its accessories did not meet the requirements of such rural magnates as the Macnamaras, who built Bunratty Castle (p. 58) in the fifteenth century. Bunratty is a fine example of a larger and grander defensible establishment. The plan is a rectangle, with four rectangular flanking turrets at the angles. On both the north and south fronts the eastern and western flanking turrets are joined, forming an attractive lofty arch which carries a room on the top storey. Donamon Castle in Co. Roscommon and Kilclief Castle in Co. Down also have the high arch spanning the flankers. At Kilclief the arch served as a machicolation.

This rectangular-block-plan with rectangular angle-turrets, used also in the fifteenth century by the Plunketts at Dunsoghly Castle in Co. Dublin (p. 110),

A major fifteenth-century castle at the level of the great hall (Bunratty)

17

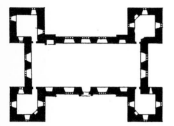

Rectangular plan with flankers, used with variations for a number of seventeenth-century strong-houses (Kanturk)

provided the model for those seventeenth-century castles more correctly described by the name by which they were known in Ireland: 'strong-houses'.

Kanturk Castle in Co. Cork (p. 144), a long oblong with square corner-towers, follows this plan. So do the castles of Burncourt in Co. Tipperary (p. 61), Monkstown in Co. Cork, and Mount Long, Co. Cork, built two or three decades later. Loughmoe Castle, Co. Tipperary, created by making additions to an earlier castle, Coppinger's Court, Co. Cork, and Ightermurrogh Castle, Co. Cork, all represent variations of the same scheme. Despite their mullioned and transomed windows which have a peaceful domestic air, there is no doubt that these castles were genuinely built with defence in mind. Their machicolations, in particular, are very evident.

Most of the planters who arrived in the late sixteenth century and the seventeenth settled down in a tower-house, but some of the wealthy opted for the comfort and style of a manor house combined with the sheltering strength of an adjoining castle. Such was 'Black Tom' of Ormond who built his gabled Elizabethan house on one side of the courtyard of his medieval castle at Carrick-on-Suir in the latter part of the sixteenth century (p. 69). It would be rash to claim this house as setting the precedent, for it seems to have been an isolated example, attributable to the personality and experience of its builder. In the seventeenth century a successful immigrant, Sir Basil Brooke, built a gabled mansion on to the medieval O'Donnell Castle at Donegal (p. 94) which he had acquired. A few years later an Irish family, the O'Briens, built a mansion on to their medieval tower at Leamaneh in Co. Clare (p. 161). In Connaught the tower-house tradition died hard: Derryhivenny Castle, Co. Galway, was built in 1643 in a bawn, with mullioned windows and rows of chimneys. Glinsk Castle in the same county (p. 122), although a larger fortified mansion, seems to have been inspired by the tower-house.

Early seventeenth-century travellers in Ireland commented on the inconveniences of the tower-houses – like Luke Gernon, describing in his *Discourse of Ireland* the hospitality he had enjoyed there:

We are come to the castle already. The castles are built very strong with narrow stayres, for security. The hall is the uppermost room, lett us go up, you shall not come down agayne till tomorrow. Take no care of your horses, they shall be sessed among the tenants. The lady of the house meets you with her trayne . . . . Salutations paste, you shall be presented with all the drinkes in the house, first the ordinary beere, then sacke, then olde-ale, the lady tastes it, you must not refuse it. The fyre is prepared in the middle of the hall, where you may sollace yourselfe till supper time, you shall not want sacke and tobacco. By this time the table is spread and plentifully furnished with variety of meates, but ill cooked and without sauce . . . They feast together with great jollyty and healths around; towards the middle of the supper, the harper begins to tune and singeth Irish rymes of auncient making. . . . Supper being ended, it is your liberty to sitt up, or to depart to your lodgeing, you shall have company in both kind. When you come to your chamber, do not expect canopy and curtaynes. It is very well if your bedd content you, and if the company be greate, you may happen to be bodkin in the middle. In the morning there will be brought unto you a cupp of aquavitae . . . it is a very wholesome drinke, and natural to digest the crudityes of the Irish feeding.

You may drink a knaggin without offence. . . . Breakfast is but the repetition of supper. When you are disposing of yourself to depart, they call for a Dogh a dores, that is, to drink at the doore, there you are presented agayne with all the drinkes in the house, as at your first entrance. Smacke them over, and lett us departe.

A French traveller, Monsieur Le Gouz de la Boullaye, writing a few years later, in 1644, was less appreciative:

The castles or houses of the nobility consist of four walls extremely high, thatched with straw; but to tell the truth, they are nothing but square towers without windows, or at least having such small apertures as to give no more light than a prison. They have little furniture, and cover their rooms with rushes, of which they make their beds in summer, and of straw in winter. They put rushes a foot deep on their floors and on their windows, and many ornament the ceilings with branches.

The greatly improved efficiency of mobile heavy artillery at the end of the sixteenth century spelled the doom of many Irish castles hitherto considered impregnable. The great cannon of the Elizabethan, and later the Cromwellian armies, breached their ancient walls. Cromwell's custom was to 'dismantle' a castle after taking it to render it useless, which he did by breaking the parapets and defensive walls. At the same time, military encounters tended more and more to take place on the battlefield, so that the importance of holding a castle to some extent waned. In Ireland, however, the continual unrest ensured continuation of the castle's popularity, both as an element in the struggle for power between the opposing parties and as protection for newcomers trying to hold their land grants against attack by the dispossessed Irish.

The castles of the early seventeenth-century immigrant potentates display a variety of plans and styles, with few common denominators save the basic defensive devices such as machicoulis and firing holes. The latter were holes pierced in the outer walls, usually covering a door, through which a musket could be fired or a lance be poked at an unwelcome visitor. In some cases the architectural origins of these castles can be traced to the styles prevailing in the place of origin of the settler, in others they are obscure. At Mallow in Co. Cork Sir Thomas Norreys built a castle (p. 174) whose plan is an oblong with polygonal flanking turrets at the front corners; a turret at the centre rear accommodated a stair and garde-robes, and a projecting turret-like wing protected the entrance. Sir Arthur Chichester's castle, Joymount, at Carrickfergus in Co. Antrim was a tall Jacobean mansion with dome-crowned projecting bays. Sir Toby Caulfield's Castle Caulfield in Co. Tyrone, generally English in character, recalls a medieval layout. Portumna Castle in Co. Galway (p. 187) was built by an Irish-born nobleman who travelled widely and lived mainly in England, which accounts for its cosmopolitan appearance.

The most distinctive settlers' castles are those of the families from Scotland, often called 'Planter's castles'. Ballygally Castle at the head of Ballgally Bay in Co. Antrim, built in 1625 by James Shaw who came from Greenock in Scotland, was constructed in a style fashionable in his native country. It has high walls, a steeply pitched roof, dormer windows and bartizans high up on the angles, supported by courses of corbelling and crowned with conical roofs. Originally two courtyards with high walls surrounded the castle. The plan is rectangular, with a flanking square tower at the north-east angle built to contain the stair which communicates with the main tower on each of its four floors. This type of castle was much favoured by the settlers in Ulster. Ballygally was inhabited by the Shaws into the nineteenth century, and continued in use as a residence into the twentieth.

Monea Castle in Co. Fermanagh (p. 176) is another building of Scots inspiration built by a native of Scotland. Its unusual chambers set diagonally on the towers with moulded courses of corbelling supporting their projecting corners can also be seen on a castle in Scotland, Claypotts, near Dundee. Castle Balfour in Co. Fermanagh (p. 73), built by a planter from Ayrshire, also has Scottish details, and was probably built, like other settlers' castles, by immigrant masons from Scotland. Killyleagh Castle in Co. Down (p. 154) is interesting not only because of its Scottish derivation, but because in the second half of the seventeenth century it was rebuilt and enlarged in the style of a medieval castle. This was an almost unique example of nostalgia for the medieval in a period when classicism was taking hold even in conservative Ireland, and gentlemen were spurning castles, finding them ugly, unfashionable and antiquated, though many had no choice but to live in them.

Classicism at the outset had ousted Gothic, but when architects tired of the limits it imposed on them they began to break away; in the 1740s one of the sources to which they looked for new forms was the Gothic. This fashion was not an academic revival of Gothic architecture, as took place in the next century, but rather a use of Gothic trimmings. To distinguish the style from the original and from the Victorian revival it is convenient to use the quaint eighteenth-century spelling, 'Gothick'. The Georgian architect who adapted Gothic elements rarely allowed them to disturb the classical symmetry of his building, nor would he use any real medieval features that would compromise the comfort of the house. Between 1750 and 1775 the taste for Gothick caught on in Ireland. The Earl of Drogheda's Moore Abbey was, it seems, the first important house to be treated in this way. It was built before Castleward in Co. Down, which has one classical front and a Gothick one topped by battlements. The leading English architects who also designed castles in Ireland, such as Wyatt, and later Nash, designed both Gothick and Neoclassical houses. As the taste for Gothick blossomed its application often went beyond a mere array of pointed windows and doors, clustered columns and plaster fan-vaulted ceilings, to include battlements, towers, turrets and mock arrow-loops. In many cases, however, the gothicization of a house consisted of little more than the castellation of its roof-line and the changing of its windows, and the best examples in Ireland of the toy-castle-look which resulted are perhaps the delightful gate-lodges of Glin Castle in Co. Limerick (p. 122), or the earlier castellated garden-house on Hillsborough Fort, which looks like a pasteboard model (p. 137).

Slane Castle in Co. Meath (XV, p. 196) is the grandest full-blown Georgian castle of the eighteenth century, and must have done much to popularize the fashion. Francis Johnston, the Irish architect who finished the work there after Wyatt, was proficient in Gothick design. He built a number of mock-castles, of which the most imposing are Markree Castle in Co. Sligo, Charleville Castle, now called Charleville Forest, in Co. Offaly, and Killeen Castle in Co. Meath (p. 152). The Pain brothers, who supervised the building of Lough

Cutra Castle (p. 170) for Nash, subsequently built a number of castles in Ireland, one well-known one being Dromoland Castle in Co. Clare, now an hotel.

At the turn of the century other styles were revived, and Tudor became popular from about 1815. It was used by Richard Morrison for Lord Meath at Kilruddery, Co. Wicklow, and for Lord Llandaff at Thomastown (p. 199). Like the Georgian Gothic, the Georgian Tudor should not be judged as an incompetent imitation. The architects deliberately chose elements that pleased them and interpreted these in combinations which they considered not only handsome but entirely licit. Consequently, even the most bogus devices are sometimes more pleasing visually than the later, more accurate, products of historicism.

As antiquarian interest grew in the nineteenth century, developing from Walter Scott Romanticism to serious study like that of Petrie and others who followed him in Ireland, so the approach to Revival architecture became more serious. W. V. Morrison's extraordinary effort at Brittas Castle in Co. Tipperary, unfortunately unfinished (p. 56), is the first fruit of this historicism in Ireland.

Charleville Castle, now Charleville Forest, Co. Offaly, one of Francis Johnston's most interesting essays in the medieval Revival style of 1800

The activities and journal of the Kilkenny and South-East of Ireland Archaeological Society, later the Royal Society of Antiquaries of Ireland, stimulated people's interest in medieval buildings. In various parts of the country enthusiasts had been repairing castles since the beginning of the century, more often than not mutilating them in the process. Now restoration work, if still sometimes heavy-handed, began to be carried out more judiciously. At Conna in Co. Cork, for example, the Reverend Alfred L'Estrange who inherited a medieval castle of the Earls of Desmond took great pains to discover what he could of its history, wrote a pamphlet on it and studied other contemporary examples before repairing it and appointing a caretaker.

When strict authenticity became the order of the day, many Victorian architects had no qualms about obliging their unfortunate clients to negotiate winding mural stairs, low doorways and long dark passages. Practically every medieval device was resurrected – dungeons, bartizans, murder-holes, moats, souterrains and machicolations. Only the medieval privy with its open chute seems to have escaped imitation. However the Victorian magnates who commissioned castles still demanded the great number of rooms and household offices that country-house living then required, so no overall medieval plan could be imitated, only individual elements. These the architect faithfully copied, and then grouped according to his fancy. Godwin's Celtic Revival extravaganza, Dromore Castle in Co. Limerick (p. 96) is an example of this method. The state of unrest in Ireland provided a golden opportunity for Godwin to reproduce genuine fortifications. In Ulster the features of the Scottish Planters' castles were revived, and Scots Baronial was popularized there by Lanyon and Lynn.

In the late nineteenth century possession of a castle signalled status and even breeding. Just as the gentleman of the early eighteenth century in Ireland had aspired to leave his medieval dwelling for a Palladian house, so the Victorian gentleman disdained his classical inheritance and developed a passionate admiration almost amounting to a mania for the medieval. In genteel Killiney, Co. Dublin, in the 1860s, even the semi-detached villa was built with castellations and turrets.

Perhaps the most authentic return to castle-dwelling was that of the aesthete Edward Martyn, who chose to live ascetically in his sixteenth-century tower-house at Tullira, Co. Galway, with sparse and simple furnishings of the period (p. 204). His friend the poet W. B. Yeats restored Ballylee Castle (p. 44) with the help of Professor William A. Scott, who also designed reproduction medieval furniture for him.

More recent restoration work, mostly by the Office of Works or the Department of the Environment in Northern Ireland, has been of a very high standard. Many of Ireland's ancient castles have been rescued from decay and oblivion, and some have been given a new life. Unfortunately, however, at least as many more are sadly neglected and the prey of vandals.

In the 1970s the lure and glamour of the 'castle look' seems not to have expired; at first sight Ballaghmore Castle in Co. Tipperary, just off the main Dublin road, four miles from Roscrea, appears to have pupped: around it have sprung up castellated bungalows and a castellated workshop.

Ballynacarriga, Co. Cork, decoration around a window on the top floor.

22

I Ballinlough Castle CO. WESTMEATH

The façade of the castellated eighteenth-century wing
seen across the ornamental lake. *See* p. 40.

II Aughnanure Castle CO. GALWAY

The stronghold of the O'Flahertys of Connemara on
the shores of Lough Corrib, built about 1500. *See* p. 36.

III Carrigafoyle Castle CO. KERRY

The stronghold of the O'Connors of Kerry on the
Shannon estuary, with a boat-dock allowing ships to
sail right inside the bawn. *See* p. 70.

IV Dundrum Castle CO. DOWN

Perhaps the most idyllically situated of all the Norman
castles in Ireland. Dundrum has one of the first
cylindrical keeps, built after it was discovered that
corners were especially vulnerable to destruction by
'picking' or 'sapping'. *See* p. 104.

Ashford Castle CO. MAYO

The archaeological and antiquarian interests of Benjamin Lee Guinness, wealthy head of the Dublin brewing firm in the mid-nineteenth century, led him to visit Connemara to inspect the ruins of the Augustinian abbey at Cong, whose cloister he eventually caused to be restored. Captivated by the extreme beauty of the shores of Lough Corrib, in 1852 he purchased lands around the abbey with the intention of building a cottage. As his interest in the region grew, he went on to buy the adjacent estate of Rosshill in 1860, and in 1864 that of Doon, which included the island ruin of Castle Kirk; later he acquired a further two thousand acres near Maan and six thousand near the Lake of Kylemore. His eldest son and heir, Sir Arthur Edward Guinness, second Baronet, accordingly found himself the landlord of twenty-seven thousand acres in Co. Galway and four thousand in Co. Mayo, including thirty-three islands in Lough Corrib and Lough Mask. Sir Arthur immediately considered building a magnate's pile which would reflect his taste, status and fortune.

The site Sir Arthur chose was on the banks of Lough Corrib, close to the ruins of Cong which had first so enchanted his father. The architect was the Kerry-born Joseph Franklin Fuller. By the end of 1870 the enormous baronial castle-style mansion had been built, incorporating a genuine medieval tower-house and complete with bridge, water-gate, towers, turrets, bartizans and cod machicolation. Within weeks Sir Arthur brought an aristocratic bride to reign over his new castle: Lady Olivia Charlotte Hedges-White, daughter of the third Earl of Bantry and an eminently suitable chatelaine. The marriage was not blessed with children, but after nine years the Queen crowned the couple's happiness by bestowing a peerage on Sir Arthur, and they became Lord and Lady Ardilaun. In 1907 the Prince of Wales, later George V, was their guest at Ashford and a special room was constructed for him.

The Victorian Revival castle built for a magnate on the shore of Lough Corrib

30

Built at a time when property and ancestry were worshipped and the outward expressions of wealth were admired above all else, Ashford in its heyday epitomized the dream of an Irish Victorian tycoon – a castle whose prestige would link his wealth and position to a feudal baronial past.

While the exterior was intended to emulate the impregnable strength of the fortress of a powerful medieval prince, the interior boasted all the opulence, technological improvements and amenities of a great late nineteenth-century country house. Besides the owners and their guests the castle had to accommodate a huge indoor staff which ranged from the butler, housekeeper and cook through a regiment of lesser servants – lady's maids, footmen, valets, parlour-maids, housemaids, stillroom maids, laundresses, kitchenmaids, scullerymaids and bootboys. The upper servants ate in the steward's room, the lower servants in the servants' hall. The outdoor staff – gardeners, coachmen, grooms and ghillies – had quarters outside the main block of buildings. Besides the hall, drawing-room, dining-room, morning-room, bedrooms and dressing-rooms, there was a boudoir, a smoking-room, a billiard room, a gun-room, a music room and a library. On the domestic side were the kitchen and sculleries, pantry, laundry with washing, airing, ironing and folding rooms, separate larders for meat, game and fish, a still-room, silver-room, brushing-room and boot-room.

After Lord Ardilaun's death in 1915 Lady Ardilaun continued to live at Ashford, and raised an obelisk on the estate to his memory. The inscription with his name and dates also extols at length Lady Ardilaun's own impeccable lineage and descent from various Earls and Dukes. After Lady Ardilaun's death the Iveagh trustees sold the castle and its contents in 1939, at an auction which lasted for two weeks. The castle where the Ardilauns and their retinue had lived in High Victorian pomp was purchased by the Irish Government, with 3,500 acres for afforestation. Later the building was resold and, renovated and enlarged, it is now a splendid hotel.

The entrance-gateway and bridge add to the effect of a medieval stronghold as conceived by a nineteenth-century architect

Askeaton Castle CO. LIMERICK

The castle of the ill-fated Earls of Desmond at Askeaton, the principal residence of the last Earls, stands on a pear-shaped island in the River Deel, once the site of a Celtic stronghold and also of an earlier medieval fortress.

The Earls of Desmond were in possession of the place from at least 1348, but the building appears to date mainly from the time of the seventh Earl, the mid-fifteenth century, and this attribution is supported by the scant documentary evidence available.

In 1583 the castle is described in a report of the Royal Commissioners on the Desmond estates as follows: 'An excellent castle formerly a chief house of the said late Earl of Desmond standing in a good state of repair, because William Pellam, Knight, Lord Chief Justiciary of Ireland, at the time of the last rebellion, remained there and repaired those parts of the same castle which the aforesaid late Earl, at the time he entered into rebellion, burned down. The said castle . . . is encircled on every side by a river running from the south to the north to the great River Shannon from which river the castle is a mile distant so that skiffs which can carry twelve tons can come to the bridge of the said castle at the springtide. The said castle contains in itself two separate courts with one bawn and several strong buildings placed here and there — namely a large hall and chamber with three cellars, a kitchen and other necessary places and bed chambers two of which have iron doors. A garden, triangular in plan, in which is a fish pond, lies to the south . . . all enclosed by a stone wall.'

The keep, 90 feet high, was built at the northern end of a grassy eminence in the upper ward. Its walls are 4 feet thick, which is unusually thin for such a building. The bailey is enclosed by a high battlemented curtain wall and defended at its southern end by a strong tower. The most interesting of the buildings is the banqueting-hall which stands in the lower ward built against the outer ramparts, on the western side overlooking the river. This is a handsome building containing a vaulted kitchen, chambers and cellar on the ground floor and a great hall above: a single room 72 feet long, 30 feet 4 inches wide at one end and 1 foot wider at the other. A blind arcade decorates the southern wall. The Decorated Gothic carving on the windows is so similar to the ornamentation in the ruined Franciscan friary near by, which was under Desmond patronage, that one must conclude that the Earls employed the same craftsmen on both buildings.

The Government wished to procure the castle as a residence for the Lord President of Munster, but was unwilling to venture force against the Earl of Desmond's garrison of 160 gallowglasses (mercenaries), 300 kerne (Irish foot-soldiers) and 30 horsemen. Negotiations for its surrender failed, and in 1579 Malby finally attacked the town, burned much of it, and desecrated the friary; but he was unable to oust the Earl, who remained secure in his stronghold. In November of that year the Earl with one thousand men at his disposal formally entered into war against the Crown. Ormond attacked with the Crown forces in December, but was still unable to capture the castle. In the spring, however, when heavy English cannon was brought to Askeaton and ranged against the castle, the garrison first wrecked some of the outbuildings and then fled.

Captain Edward Berkeley from Somerset was sent to take command of Askeaton Castle, and remained as Constable for nine years. His brother Francis was then granted Askeaton as the Manor of Rock Barkley at an annual rent of £87.10s., with the obligation to erect houses for over fifty English families: four for freeholders, three for farmers and forty-six for copyholders. The castle was not included in the grant, being reserved to the Crown.

In 1599 the Earl of Essex came to the relief of the garrison at Askeaton which had then been besieged for 147 days by the Irish. There he knighted Francis Berkeley, who, as Sir Francis, at length received the grant of the castle in 1611, when he offered to wall the town and make the castle a place of refuge for the English. Since the Battle of Kinsale he had kept a garrison of 150 at Askeaton. He proved to be a popular landlord, permitting Irish husbandmen to live on his lands and bringing Irish-speaking Protestant ministers to the parish.

The Manor descended through a Berkeley heiress to the Taylors of Ballynort, but the castle was seized by the Irish and dismantled by the Parliamentarian Captain Axtell when he took it in 1652. The Earl of Orrery, convinced of its potential usefulness, tried to persuade the Government to refit it, but it was not repaired, and fell into disuse. It is now a National Monument.

The fifteenth-century tower and gabled end of the splendid Desmond banqueting-hall rising above the curtain wall

Aughnanure Castle CO. GALWAY

Above, *the banqueting-hall built within the castle compound in the sixteenth century and then probably roofed with thatch.* Right, *vine scrolls decorating a window, a favourite motif in Ireland at the period. See Colour Plate II*

To judge from its appearance, Aughnanure Castle on the banks of lovely Lough Corrib, about two miles from Oughterard, was built about the end of the fifteenth or the beginning of the sixteenth century. It was then the stronghold of the O'Flahertys of Connemara. The castle stands on a rocky promontory between the two branches of a stream which flowed into the lake, and originally the site was surrounded by water on all three sides. The entrance to the castle is by a natural bridge of rock.

The six-storey tower, 40 feet by 28 feet, is well built and widely battered at the base. The important fireplace in the third-floor chamber indicates that this was the principal apartment; at that level on the entrance front of the castle there are two corner bartizans. The fourth floor has a vaulted ceiling. The parapets with machicolations on all four sides command a superb view of Lough Corrib and over to the distant Joyce mountains. The roof is a good modern reconstruction.

An unusual feature at Aughnanure is the double bawn. Both the inner and outer baileys have a turret at the south-west corner. From the roof of the inner turret a sentry might command a view of the whole compound and the outer bawn wall. A detached banqueting-hall was built against the outer wall in the sixteenth century, and although it is now ruinous, some of the walls having collapsed, we can see from the decorative motif on the window jambs and soffits – a vine with clusters of grapes – that it had pretensions to style.

The castle was attacked by Sir Edward Fitton in 1572 when the Crown was endeavouring to impose its authority in Connaught, but Hugh O'Flaherty managed to secure his interest in his patrimonial estate by a Royal grant of the castle and lands in the reign of James I. Aughnanure's key position guarding the head of the lake was of particular importance during the Cromwellian blockade of Galway.

The O'Flahertys lost their estates in the Cromwellian confiscations and failed to retrieve them under the ungrateful Stuarts, to whom they had been loyal. The heir, Roderick O'Flaherty, the historian of Corrib, recited the tale of the misfortune: 'This was my natal soil and patrimony through a long series of ancestors. It was a manor exempted by patent from Royal tribute, endowed with the privilege of holding a market and fairs, and honoured with the liberty of a seneschal's court to settle litigation. But having lost my father before I was two years of age, I came under the tutelary protection of the King by the laws of the country regulating minors, and paid, as was the custom, money for my wardship, but before it was lawful for me to enter upon the enjoyment of my patrimonial inheritance, I lost the patronage of my guardian by the regicidal execution of my King in the nineteenth year of my age, and the royal heir (the prince) half a year younger than I, was forced to seek refuge in a foreign country. The Lord has wonderfully restored the prince to his Kingdom, by the consent of all good men without contention of blood, but He has not found me worthy to be restored to the Kingdom of my cottage. Against thee, O Lord, only have I sinned. Blessed be the name of the Lord for ever.'

In the nineteenth century the castle was once again the property of an O'Flaherty. Edmund O'Flaherty of the Leconfield branch of the family planted yew-trees about the castle in the 1850s to perpetuate the derivation of its name from the Irish, 'the field of the yews'. The castle is now a National Monument.

Ballingarry Castle CO. LIMERICK

Ballingarry occupied a strategic position in the pass through the hills that stretch nearly from the Deel to the Maigue separating north and south Connello, a natural gateway used since ancient times by the indigenous tribes. It became of importance during the trouble-fraught English rule in Munster. Already in 1408 we find Henry IV sanctioning a payment to wall the town because 'the greater part thereof has been destroyed by Irish foes and English rebels'. Town and castle were then in the possession of the de Lesse or de Lacy family, whose association with Ballingarry dates from the beginning of the fourteenth century at least. The castle as we see it today was built in the fifteenth century, when the Earls of Desmond held undisputed sway over the region, and following the destruction of 1408. Its tall, slender battlemented tower is both strong and elegant.

The de Lacys were united to the Earls of Desmond by bonds of marriage, tradition, politics and faith, and from the beginning of the Desmond wars they sided with the rebels. Ballingarry Castle was one of those which Captain John Ward reported to Cecil he had reduced in his campaign of 1569, when the men of the garrison were butchered. After the defeat of the Earl of Desmond in 1583, John de Lacy forfeited the castle, but later he was pardoned for his complicity and reinstated. Later again, Connello was divided into seigniories, and in 1607 the castle and lands were surrendered by John de Lacy to the adventurer Richard Boyle, first Earl of Cork, though the de Lacy family seems to have remained in residence. On 19 May 1630 the Earl leased the castle, impropriate rectory and tithes to David de Lacy, son of John, for 'seventy-five pounds of good and lawful money of England, pure sylver without misture' annually.

David was bound to hand over the premises in good repair on the expiry of the twenty-one-year lease. The Earl reserved the patronage of the living to himself, however, granting it to his cousin, Richard Boyle, later Bishop of Cork. The de Lacys managed to survive at Ballingarry until 1654, when the Civil Survey shows William Lacie *alias* 'Lacie of Ballingarry', an Irish papist, as proprietor of Ballingarry Castle.

Like most of the Catholic landowners, the de Lacys were eventually swept away in favour of landlords loyal to the English interest. In 1667 the Castle and lands were awarded to Major John Odell, who had suffered losses elsewhere in the county in the Rising of 1641. He came to live at the castle with his wife and children, serving as High Sheriff of the County in 1678–9. After his petition to the Government to fit up and fortify Ballingarry Castle was rejected he built a mansion near by in 1685.

The castle may have suffered when the town of Ballingarry was burned by the Jacobites in 1691, but it continued occupied, frequently by the parson as there was no glebe house until 1822. It was known locally as Parson's Castle. In 1820 during the Rockite troubles it served as a barracks, and then as a sick-bay during the cholera epidemic. In the mid-nineteenth century, when Castle Lane was a fashionable quarter, Dr Robert Odell lived in the old castle for many years with his wife and children. Ballingarry is now a sleepy depopulated village, and its castle a cowhouse.

The elegant ruined tower of the de Lacy castle, built in the early fifteenth century

Ballinlough Castle CO. WESTMEATH

Ballinlough has long been in the possession of one family, the O'Reillys, direct ancestors in the male line of the present owner, Sir Hugh Nugent, sixth Baronet, whose great-great-grandfather the first Baronet, Sir Hugh O'Reilly, adopted his mother's maiden surname of Nugent upon inheriting the property of a rich maternal uncle in 1812. It is not clear exactly when this branch of the O'Reilly family, which claims descent from the ancient lords of East Breffny, moved eastward and acquired Ballinlough. A stone inserted in the front of the castle bears the date 1618 with the O'Reilly arms and crest, and the initials J O'R, possibly of a John or James O'Reilly. It is probable that Ballinlough came to the O'Reillys through a

The seat of a Catholic gentry family which managed to survive the confiscations of Penal times. See Colour Plate I

marriage into the Nugent family in the sixteenth century, for these lands were once part of the estates of the Nugents of Delvin.

The castle of 1618 was built on the site of a medieval stronghold. A small tower at the back and vestiges of the ancient walls survive. The 1618 building in turn was incorporated into a later building early in the eighteenth century, with a front and doorway in the classical style then popular. The impressive entrance-hall is two storeys high, overlooked by a gallery with an elegant balustrade and a finely carved frieze. On this frieze a particularly Irish motif, the mask, appears among the swirls of foliage.

Much later in the century, James O'Reilly, who died in 1786, added a new wing on the north-west side of the original building, butted on to the thick wall of the old castle. This contains two handsome ground-floor reception-rooms with large windows looking over the lake. The dining-room has a fine door-surround and plasterwork in the manner of Wyatt, and, as the drawing-room has a splendid marble mantelpiece identical to one known to be by Wyatt at Curraghmore, it would seem that Wyatt himself made designs for James O'Reilly.

The castellated circular turrets at the angles of the new wing, communicating with the reception-rooms, are the same in plan as those added to Malahide Castle by James O'Reilly's daughter Margaret, wife of Richard Talbot of Malahide. It is evident that the designs at Ballinlough and Malahide are connected: it has been suggested that both were the work of Wogan Browne of Clongowes Castle, an amateur architect and a kinsman of the Talbots.

The O'Reillys of Ballinlough were among the few Irish families who contrived to keep both their estates and their Catholic faith during the period of the Penal Laws in the eighteenth century. The younger sons sought careers and fortune in military service on the Continent – one, Count Andrew O'Reilly (1742–1832), became Governor-General of Vienna – and it was as a result of these connections abroad that some fine foreign furniture came to Ballinlough.

Anthony Atkinson who visited Ballinlough in 1815 reported his favourable impressions in *The Irish Tourist*:

'The castle and demesne of Ballinlough had an appearance of antiquity highly gratifying to my feelings . . . I reined in my horse within a few perches of the grand gate of Ballinlough to take a view of the castle: it stands on a little eminence above a lake which beautifies the demesne; and not only the structure of the castle, but the appearance of the trees, and even the dusky colour of the gate and walls, as you enter, contribute to give the whole scenery an appearance of antiquity, while the prospect is calculated to infuse into the heart of the beholder, a mixed sentiment of veneration and delight.

'Having visited the castle of Ballinlough, the interior of which appears a good deal modernized, Sir Hugh had the politeness to shew me two or three of the principal apartments: these, together with the gallery in the hall, had as splendid an appearance as any thing which I had, until that time, witnessed in private buildings. The rooms are furnished in a stile – I cannot pretend to estimate the value, either of the furniture or ornamental works, but some idea thereof may be formed from the expence of a fine marble chimney-piece . . . five hundred pounds sterling, a sum that would establish a country tradesman in business! The collection of paintings . . . must have been purchased at an immense expence also . . .'

The present owner and his wife have restored the castle with care; they have added more fine pieces to its contents, including some from the sale of the contents of Malahide Castle in 1976, and they have improved the attractive demesne.

The handsome carved frieze of the gallery with masks, a favourite Irish motif, among the foliage

Ballintober Castle CO. ROSCOMMON

Ballintober became the principal seat of the O'Conors, the royal family of Connaught, after the Anglo-Norman invasion of Ireland at the end of the twelfth century. Since the Irish rulers had no tradition in stone castle-building, the O'Conors chose to build their castle to a plan borrowed from the invaders. Their nearest example was at Roscommon. It is not known exactly when the O'Conors built Ballintober, but it was near the end of the thirteenth century, shortly after they had captured Roscommon Castle and held it for a few years. Ballintober is first mentioned in the Annals in 1311, and then again in 1315 when the leader of a rebellious sept of the O'Conors seized it in the absence of the chief. From 1385 until it was confiscated in the seventeenth century, Ballintober was the seat of the O'Conor Don, the head of one branch of the great clan.

The plan of the building is a near-rectangle with asymmetrical polygonal towers at the four corners. The imposing south-western tower and the south-eastern tower are hexagonal, the north-eastern tower is heptagonal, and the great north-western tower, which was partially rebuilt and repaired in 1627, is a pentagon. All the towers had residential apartments in the upper storeys. They are linked by a high and massive curtain wall which enclosed the spacious courtyard, 170 feet by 237 feet. The entrance was on the east side, protected by projecting flanking turrets. A broad ditch around the whole castle afforded further protection.

In 1585, having compounded, the O'Conor Don surrendered his estate to the Crown and had it regranted by a Royal patent which specifically included the 'castle, bawne, and lands of Ballintuber'. His loyalty to the English brought him the enmity of the northern rebels, however, so that he was obliged to surrender Ballintober in 1598 to the O'Donnell, who attacked it with cannon and breached the walls. After peace had been restored the O'Conor Don, who had been knighted by the Earl of Essex, was able to repossess his castle, and was given a new grant of it by James I in 1617. Sir Hugh remained loyal, but his castle became the rendezvous of the Catholic gentry, whose dissatisfaction mounted until in 1624 it approached insurrection point. The Lord Deputy received a report in that year that over eighty priests had assembled to confer at Ballintober Castle one Wednesday, armed with swords, daggers and pistols, along with a number of gentlemen, also armed, and each attended by two armed servants. The O'Conor Don and his family had been present.

When eventually the Irish Catholic forces were organized, in 1641, Charles O'Conor Don, who had succeeded his father Sir Hugh, was colonel of a regiment. The Parliamentarians under Coote and Eardley routed the Irish who were superior in number but poorly armed; however they made no attack on Ballintober Castle for fear that it was held by a large garrison. For his part in the rebellion Charles O'Conor Don lost his lands when the victorious Parliamentarians meted out punishment. After his death his widow was allotted seven hundred acres near the castle, but the castle itself was assigned to persons transplanted by Cromwell from other parts of Ireland. Hugh, the next O'Conor Don, never officially retrieved the castle under Charles II, but his son, another Hugh, had castle and lands adjudged to him by decree in 1677. He mortgaged his estate, the mortgage changed hands and the reversionary interest was inherited by an heir who was a Catholic and therefore disqualified under the Penal Laws. A lengthy wrangle ensued, culminating in an act of bravado in 1786, when one of the claimants, Alexander O'Conor of Clonalis, later the O'Conor Don, marched to Ballintober with his retainers, proclaimed himself the rightful owner, and, being recognized as such by the tenantry, took possession of the castle and collected the rents. The neighbouring Protestant gentry were greatly alarmed, fearing that this might be the beginning of a move by the descendants of the old Irish landlords to repossess their sequestered ancestral estates. The Government was alerted and O'Conor was forcibly ejected by the authorities. In 1789 the trustees of the other claimants were enabled by a private Act of Parliament to dispose of the contested castle and lands. They sold them to Maurice Mahon of Strokestown, later the first Baron Hartland. The castle is now a National Monument.

One of the massive polygonal towers of the castle of the O'Conors, once rulers of Connaught

Ballylee Castle CO. GALWAY

The sixteenth-century tower-house of the Burkes in the barony of Kiltartan which became the home of the poet W. B. Yeats

W. B. Yeats chose the Irish name 'Thoor Ballylee' for his tower-house beside the Cloon River in Co. Galway in order, as he wrote in a letter, to 'keep people from suspecting us of modern gothic and a deer park'. Previously he had addressed his letters from 'Ballylee Castle, Gort', and referred proudly to his not-long-acquired tower as 'my castle'.

Yeats first saw Ballylee in the summer of 1896 when he was a guest of Edward Martyn at Tullira, and wrote of it three years later: 'I have been lately to a little group of houses, not many enough to be called a village, in the barony of Kiltartan in County Galway, whose name, Ballylee, is known through all the west of Ireland. There is the old square castle, Ballylee, inhabited by a farmer and his wife, and a cottage where their daughter and son-in-law live, and a little mill with an old miller, and old ash trees throwing green shadows upon a little river and great stepping-stones. I went there two or three times last year to talk to the miller about Biddy Early, a wise woman that lived in Clare some years ago, and about her saying "There is a cure for all evil between the two mill-wheels of Ballylee," and to find out from him or another whether she meant the moss between the running waters or some other herb. I have been there this summer and I shall be there again before it is autumn, because Mary Hynes, a beautiful woman whose name is still a wonder by turf fires, died there sixty years ago, for our feet would linger where beauty has lived its life of sorrow to make us understand that it is not of the world.'

After his first visit in 1896, Yeats spent almost every summer for twenty years as a guest of his friend Lady Gregory at Coole Park, only three miles from Ballylee. His enchantment with the medieval tower persisted, and in 1916 he purchased the property for £35 from the Congested Districts Board. It had been acquired with parts of the Gregory estate for redistribution, but nobody had wanted the ruinous tower and the two cottages attached to it. From the outset Yeats' intention was to live there within walking distance of his friends Lady Gregory at Coole Park and Edward Martyn at Tullira Castle, but this was not the only attraction of Ballylee. It also appealed to Yeats' liking for the life and surroundings of a cultured aristocracy, his appreciation of leisurely peace, of rural tradition and history; he described it as 'a place full of history and romance'.

Ballylee, like Martyn's Tullira, was originally one of the fortresses of the ubiquitous Clanrickarde Burkes, built in the sixteenth century. It was known as Islandmore Castle when it belonged to Edward Ulick Burke, who died in 1597. Twenty years later the proprietor was Richard Burke, Earl of Clanrickarde, the builder of Portumna Castle. Yeats liked to imagine the warlike Burke clansmen of that time; in *The Tower*, a collection of a number of poems written at and about Ballylee, he wrote:

> Before that ruin came, for centuries,
> Rough men-at-arms, cross-gartered to the knees
> Or shod in iron, climbed the narrow stairs,
> And certain men-at-arms there were

Whose images, in the Great Memory stored,
Come with loud cry and panting breast
To break upon a sleeper's rest
While their great wooden dice beat on the board.

Mostly with money earned by his lecture-tours Yeats repaired Ballylee, first the roof and then the fabric. His architect was Professor William A. Scott, who also designed furniture for the apartments which were made habitable floor by floor. Yeats followed the work of the architect and the local artisans with keen interest. His marriage in 1917 increased his haste to complete the work. In the summer of 1918 he wrote in a letter the lines he intended to have inscribed on a great stone beside the front door:

I, the poet, William Yeats,
With common sedge and broken slates
And smithy work from the Gort forge,
Restored this tower for my wife George:
And on my heirs I lay a curse
If they should alter for the worse,
From fashion or an empty mind,
What Raftery built and Scott designed.

Yeats later reworked this poem, and it appears now on a stone set up at Ballylee by the board of the Abbey Theatre, Dublin, in its final form:

I, the poet William Yeats,
With old millboards and sea-green slates,
And smithy work from the Gort forge,
Restored this tower for my wife George,
And may these characters remain
When all is ruin once again.

Yeats and his wife were blissfully happy at Ballylee. He described the place in his poem 'My House':

An ancient bridge, and a more ancient tower,
A farmhouse that is sheltered by its wall,
An acre of stony ground,
Where the symbolic rose can break in flower,
Old ragged elms, old thorns innumerable,
The sound of the rain or sound
Of every wind that blows;
The stilted water-hen
Crossing stream again
Scared by the splashing of a dozen cows;
A winding stair, a chamber arched with stone,
A grey stone fireplace with an open hearth,
A candle and a written page.
Il Penseroso's Platonist toiled on

In some like chamber, shadowing forth
How the daemonic rage
Imagined everything.
Benighted travellers
From markets and from fairs
Have seen his midnight candle glimmering.

Writing in the ground-floor chamber, Yeats called it 'the pleasantest room I have yet seen, a great wide window opening over the river and a round arched door leading to the thatched hall . . .' He loved the mural stair, too, and wrote to a friend: 'Stone stairs to my surprise are the most silent of all stairs.' In 1926 Yeats still wrote of Ballylee as 'this blessed place'; but in the ensuing years his commitments prevented him from spending much time there, and especially after Lady Gregory's death in 1932 he was disinclined to go there. The ruin he had foreseen set in, but Bord Failte, encouraged by the Kiltartan Society, restored the castle as a Yeats memorial and opened it to the public in 1965 for the centenary of the poet's birth. Mrs Yeats and her son and daughter have made the property over to a trust. The walls have been repainted in the colours chosen by Yeats and Scott. Some of the furniture designed by Scott was discovered and brought back, and other pieces have been made by a local artisan to the original designs.

The window of the poet's simple bedchamber

Ballysaggartmore

CO. WATERFORD

Arthur Keily, a Waterford gentleman whose ambition was greater than his fortune, was seized with the desire to be in fashion and build a castle of historic appearance on his estate near Lismore. It is said, too, that his wife, as proud and ambitious as he, was anxious to outshine her sister-in-law, Mrs John Keily, the chatelaine of Strancally Castle, built by the architects James and George Richard Pain above the Blackwater in the early 1820s. The work on Mr and Mrs Arthur Keily's dream-castle began with the approach, a splendid gateway with the lodge in the turrets, the avenue, a bridge and an inner gateway and lodge. When these had been completed Mr Keily's funds were exhausted and so the castle was never built. The fabulous gates lead only to an insignificant little house where the Keilys continued to live, perhaps regretful of their folly, or perhaps satisfied by the grandeur of their gate.

The gate-house of the castle-that-never-was

46

Belfast Castle CO. ANTRIM

Above, corbelled bartizan and crow-stepped gable of the massive tower, built in the Scots Baronial style to express Ulster's links with Scotland. In contrast, right, is the Italianate serpentine stair added on the garden front (detail)

The first Belfast Castle, a tall sixteenth-century fortified manor house in the town, was destroyed by fire in 1708. Subsequently the Earls of Donegall (later Marquesses), once the sole proprietors of Belfast, lived mainly in England as spendthrift absentee landlords and had no seat on their Irish estates. Their extravagance culminated in the sale of these estates through the Incumbered Estates Court, after the second Marquess had died in 1844 leaving debts of over £400,000.

His son and successor, the third Marquess, was then a man in middle age, living with his family in an unpretentious house called Ormeau in the suburbs of the city. Despite his straitened circumstances, upon remarrying in 1862 the third Marquess determined to build an important castle in his deer park on Cave Hill, a superb site outside the city overlooking Belfast

Lough. The Donegall fortune had dwindled so drastically that the Marquess was unable to underwrite the costs of the building work, and the project was rescued by his rich son-in-law, who having married the Marquess's only surviving child stood to inherit what remained of the unentailed estates. This was Lord Ashley, son of the seventh Earl of Shaftesbury, the eminent philanthropist; he guaranteed the amount, which was optimistically estimated by the Donegall trustees at £11,000. The building had first been announced in 1865, but the protracted financial arrangements delayed the commencement of work until 1867. By the time the castle was completed in 1870 the cost had far exceeded the estimate.

The Marquess and Marchioness had much admired Castle View House at Cahir, Co. Tipperary, built for the Marquess's sister-in-law the Countess of Glengall in 1862 by the Belfast firm of Lanyon and Lynn, and designed by W. H. Lynn. Accordingly the commission for Belfast Castle went to the same firm. Sir Charles Lanyon, the senior partner, President of the Royal Institute of Architects in Ireland, architect, politician and property speculator, has been given credit for Belfast Castle, but the design was made and executed by the skilled junior partner, W. H. Lynn, who was then at the peak of his successful career.

The Prince Consort had set the fashion for castellated mansions in the Scottish Baronial manner with the fanciful reconstruction by William Smith of Balmoral Castle in Aberdeenshire in 1853. Intellectual and aesthetic values were subordinated to a romantic nostalgia, producing a showy mixture of gables and turrets with strangely contrived proportions. Although less sentimental and romantic than the Royal prototype, Belfast with its massive six-storey tower, crow-stepped gables, conical turrets and restless skyline is an uninhibited offspring of Balmoral.

Lynn abandoned his usually balanced synthesis in some features at Belfast Castle. The porch is an uneasy combination of Doric columns and bogus-looking strapwork; two gaunt bow-windows sit spuriously on curved courses of corbelling heavily carved with foliage and flowers. Lynn was not responsible, however, for the most surprising exterior feature of the castle, an elaborate Italianate baroque serpentine stair on the garden front which connects the reception-rooms with the garden-terrace below. This stair was built in 1894 by the ninth Earl of Shaftesbury to indulge a whim of his mother, the Dowager Countess.

The ninth Earl of Shaftesbury, one-time Mayor of the city, presented the castle to the Corporation of Belfast in 1934. It is now used for civic functions.

Birr Castle CO. OFFALY

The medieval stronghold of the O'Carrolls was sited about 180 feet to the north-west of the present castle at Birr. It became the seat of the senior branch of the clan in 1532 after internal disputes which eventually served to undermine the strength of this family, the one-time rulers of Ely O'Carroll, a territory covering about 160 square miles.

In 1537 Lord Leonard Grey, the Lord Deputy, took Birr Castle and secured the submission of the Chief, who was subsequently granted a peerage as Baron of Ely. However the O'Carrolls continued to attack the Pale periodically and to fight among themselves, as well as conducting forays against the Butlers and the English. In 1619 the Government seized an oppor-

The great gate of the inner gate-house displays the full heraldic achievement of the Earls of Rosse

tunity, the death of Sir Charles O'Carroll, to declare the territory Crown property and assign it for Plantation. Much of the land was regranted to the former Irish owners, but dispersed among them were new English settlers whose presence, it was hoped, would bring stability to the region. Birr Castle and over one thousand acres of land were thus allotted to Sir Laurence Parsons, an ambitious and intelligent adventurer who had served as Attorney-General for Munster.

Sir Laurence at once set about renovating and enlarging the O'Carroll castle as a suitable residence. He erected or rebuilt an important gate-house with flanking free-standing towers. Steadily enlarged over the years and amalgamated with the flankers, this gate-house has become the core of the present castle; it forms the hall, reached by a flight of stone steps at the centre of the building. The vaulted basement below was the archway-entrance of Sir Laurence's gatehouse.

Sir Laurence's son, Sir William Parsons, Governor of Ely O'Carroll, lost Birr during the stormy years of the Civil War. In 1642 the castle was attacked by the Irish and defended by Parsons with thirty-five horsemen and Captain Coote with one hundred foot soldiers, raised and armed by themselves. When Birr was again besieged in January 1643, Sir William was forced to capitulate and surrender it. However in 1650 the Parliamentarians under General Ireton wrested the castle from the Confederate Catholics, who set fire to it before leaving.

After the war Sir William's son, another Laurence, was able to return to Birr Castle and set about the work of repair. He was created a Baronet in 1677. In 1689, Sir Laurence, who had blockaded himself in the castle with a party of neighbours, was forced out and tried for high treason on the grounds that he was holding it for William of Orange, whereas it appears that he was defending himself against his agent, a Jacobite, who hoped to seize the place and keep it for himself. The Williamites arrived, saved Sir Laurence and garrisoned the castle. It was then attacked with heavy cannon by Irish Jacobites under the young Duke of Berwick. The besieged garrison was reduced to making improvised bullets out of a lead cistern, but somehow managed to hold out until the Jacobites raised the siege. The castle was then appropriated for several months by the Williamite army for use as a military hospital.

In 1778 Sir William Parsons demolished the ancient tower, and at about the same time dredged the lake, laid out the park and planted many fine trees and shrubs in the gardens. Successive owners of Birr continued to improve the demesne, and the present Earl and Countess, enthusiastic and knowledgeable gardeners, have worked tirelessly for over forty years to bring the gardens to their present perfection. The estate is now one of the showplaces of Ireland, and is open to the public. The River Garden, the Lagoon Garden, the Formal Gardens, the High Walk, the Arboretum and the River Walk vie in enchanting the visitor – here intense, dramatic and brilliant, there delightfully sentimental and romantic.

A giant gunnera in the waters of the castle's extensive gardens

The porch of the nineteenth-century castle built over the medieval gateway

The present appearance of the castle is due to the interest and enterprise of that Sir Laurence Parsons, later second Earl of Rosse, whom Wolfe Tone considered one of the few honest men in the Irish House of Commons. A bitter opponent of the Union, an enlightened and liberal-minded patriot, an intellectual and cosmopolitan man of many parts, Sir Laurence devoted time, thought and money to the improvement of his estate, including the town of Birr

and the castle. In 1801 he was busy with an architect named John Johnston, planning and designing the improvements. Some of his notebooks with sketches survive; they include one of the Gothick-style entrance gate, built as it there appears. The front of the existing house was embellished, refaced and gothicized, and additions were made including the splendid Gothick reception-room on the side overlooking the River Camcor. Later, in 1832 after a fire had damaged the roof, the central block was raised one storey and rebattlemented.

A battlemented and turretted stone building in the park was erected as a frame for the large telescope constructed between 1842 and 1845 by the third Earl.

Blackrock Castle CO. CORK

The Lord Deputy Mountjoy built a castle at Blackrock in 1604 to protect the passage up the River Lee to the city of Cork from the harbour. Subsequently the ownership of the castle was vested in the Corporation, and the Mayor of Cork, being also the Admiral of the Port since 1627, held an Admiralty Court there. Once a year on 1 August, to commemorate their jurisdiction over the creeks and strands, the mayor and aldermen went out in boats to the high-water mark and other points on the channel. Afterwards, a public entertainment was held in the castle at the expense of the city. In 1722 the Corporation spent £296 on improving the old building, and constructed a handsome octagonal room in the tower.

The castle on the River Lee where the mayors of Cork entertained

Elegantly situated on a promontory, the castle as it is seen today is the result of a rebuilding by the brothers James and George Richard Pain in 1829. They received this commission from the City Fathers, as the old castle had been seriously damaged by fire and was unusable. It consists of a bold circular tower with a turret and a water-gate built of local cut-limestone. At first it was assigned to the mayor as a summer residence. The topographer Samuel Lewis writing in 1837 admired its banqueting-room.

The castle is now a popular restaurant.

Blarney Castle CO. CORK

Blarney is perhaps the best known of all Irish castles; its name has passed into the English language both as a noun meaning smoothly flattering or cajoling talk, and as a transitive verb meaning to assail with flattery or to use flattering speech. Crofton Croker, the early nineteenth-century antiquarian, claimed to have elucidated the origin of this usage in the everlasting unfulfilled promises of Cormac MacDermot Mac-Carthy, the chatelain of Blarney in the closing years of the reign of Elizabeth I. MacCarthy, having promised to deliver his castle to Carew, the Lord President of Munster, endlessly delayed actually doing so, placating him with soft talk which came to be dubbed 'Blarney talk'. An unlikely embroidery on these circumstances would have it that the old Queen herself, exasperated by the procrastination, petulantly exclaimed: 'Blarney, Blarney, I will hear no more of this Blarney!'

The tradition which attributes to a stone of the castle the power to endow whoever kisses it with sweet persuasive eloquence was popularized in the last century by Father Prout in a song-poem published in his *Reliques* in 1860:

> There is a stone there
> That whoever kisses
> Oh! he never misses
> To grow eloquent.
> 'Tis he may clamber
> To a lady's chamber
> Or become a Member
> Of Parliament.
> A clever spouter
> He'll sure turn out, or
> An out and outer
> To be let alone.
> Don't hope to hinder him
> Sure he's a pilgrim
> From the Blarney Stone.

The now famous Blarney Stone, the stone of eloquence, is on one of the parapets. To kiss it one has to lie on one's back and be lowered head downwards over the edge of the wall.

The castle appears as an L-shaped building, with a slender tower containing a stair and small rooms, on to which has been added, overlapping it, a massive four-storey keep, battered and battlemented, with machicolations carried on elegant tapering corbels. This latter building has been attributed to Cormac Laidir MacCarthy of Muskerry in 1446, and the date is consistent with its appearance. After Cormac died in 1494 his heirs continued in strength and style at Blarney, where in the sixteenth century they could raise three thousand fighting men. The MacCarthys retained the castle after Cormac MacDermot MacCarthy's protracted dealings with Elizabeth I's ministers, but lost it in the Civil War when they adhered staunchly to the Royalist cause. After taking it, Lord Broghill made Blarney his headquarters.

On the Restoration the Lord of Muskerry was rewarded for his loyalty by Charles II, restored to his estate and granted a peerage as Viscount Muskerry and Earl of Clancarty. Donogh, the fourth Earl, his grandson, was brought up in England as a Protestant, but he abjured, returned to the old faith, and espoused the cause of James II when the King landed at Kinsale in 1689. While the Jacobite cause went well, Blarney Castle was used as a prison for the Protestants of Cork, but when Cork fell to the Williamites in 1690 the Earl of Clancarty was taken prisoner and forfeited his estates. He went into exile and died at Hamburg in 1734. There is a tradition that before leaving Blarney the Earl hid his chest of silver plate there, perhaps in the lake, and that his ghost returns to seek it.

The estate was bought by the Hollow Sword Blades Company of London, and Rowland Davies, Dean of Cork, lived there as their tenant. It is recounted that when he had to leave after the castle had been sold in 1703, he took off with him enough materials to build his own new house. The purchaser of Blarney was Sir Richard Pyne, the Lord Chief Justice, but he disposed of it almost immediately to Sir James Jefferyes who had been appointed Governor of Cork in 1698. Sir James lived for the remainder of his life at Blarney. His grandson built a Gothick-style mansion against the east side of the old castle.

The castle and its splendidly adorned gardens, with statues and a picturesque pseudo-megalith, were a showplace in the eighteenth century, admired by painters and poets. The poet Millikin wrote:

> The Muses shed a tear
> When the cruel auctioneer
> With a hammer in his hand
> To sweet Blarney came.

The Jefferyes heiress brought Blarney to her husband Sir George Conway Colthurst, fifth Baronet, and it is now the residence of their great-granddaughter Mrs Hillyard, *née* Colthurst. The old castle and grounds are open to the public.

The castle built in the fifteenth century by the MacCarthys of Muskerry

Brittas Castle CO. TIPPERARY

A view of Brittas Castle with battlemented round turrets and a high bawn wall, and described as 'The seat of Henry Grace Langley', appears in the *Memoirs of the Family of Grace* by Sheffield Grace, published in 1823. The medieval castle of the Butlers of Brittas had come into the Grace family possession with the marriage of Henry's maternal great-grandfather to a Butler heiress. Tradition has it that this large old castle was badly damaged by fire, and that the remains were pulled down. Only the bases of the towers can still be seen today. The property passed on the death of Henry Grace Langley to his nephew Captain Henry Augustus Langley, who employed William Vitruvius Morrison to build a new castle.

According to the biographer of that talented but neurotic architect, the design of the new castle was 'by the desire of the proprietor both in form and proportions that of the ancient English Baronial castle of the earlier period'. He added that 'the building, owing to the sudden death of Captain Langley, was never completed'. This is confirmed by the topographer Samuel Lewis, who reported in 1837 that 'Brittas Castle, the property of the Langley family, was commenced on a very extensive scale by the late Captain Langley, but remains in an unfinished state.' The unfortunate Captain had been killed by masonry falling from a tripod during the building work in 1834, and his heirs apparently lacked the money, the desire, or the ambition to continue the construction. The cousin who inherited Brittas died within weeks, while his eldest son and heir was still a minor. Brittas was sold, although it is now once again owned by a member of the Langley family.

Morrison's building consists of a truly formidable barbican tower with a lofty arch over the entrance. Below it a moat which may have survived from the medieval stronghold and been put back in service. It still holds water.

Unfortunately Morrison's designs for the rest of the castle have not been found, but it is clear that his plan was for a meticulous large-scale reproduction of an important medieval castle. Various places have been suggested as his model, but plainly the intention was to follow the ground-plan of the older castle on the site.

Right, a nineteenth-century exercise in historical authenticity, this project of a Tipperary gentleman never advanced beyond the massive barbican tower. Below, the moat beneath the entrance

Bunratty Castle CO. CLARE

Above, *the table in the solar, reputedly made from timbers of an Armada ship; and* right, *the imposing fifteenth-century castle of the great Earls of Thomond*

The site of Bunratty was once an island, and was of great strategic importance in medieval times because it commanded a view of water-traffic passing to and from the port of Limerick. The Anglo-Norman Robert de Muscegros built a fortification on the summit of the islet in the thirteenth century. This fort was probably little more than a wooden tower mounted on a flat-topped mound overlooking the surrounding area, where the tidal waters of the Shannon covered what are now roads and farmlands. Subsequently Bunratty passed to Sir Thomas de Clare who built a stone castle there in 1277. Such was the importance of the place that a thriving town grew up around the castle. The Irish of Thomond defeated and slew Sir Richard de Clare, son of Sir Thomas, in 1318. When they reached Bunratty to take possession they found it abandoned: Sir Richard's widow had burned down both castle and town before fleeing by boat to England, and the townspeople, more than a thousand in number, mostly English settlers, had deserted the place. Twice the King's men recaptured and repaired Bunratty, but each time they were unable to hold it. By the middle of the fifteenth century the Macnamaras of Clann Cuilein were firmly established there.

The building of the present imposing castle, erected about 1450 not far from the earlier one, is ascribed to Maccon MacSioda Macnamara and his son Sean Finn, who died in 1467. The castle passed into the possession of the O'Briens, possibly through the marriage of Tirlogh O'Brien, Prince of Thomond, who died in 1528, to Raghnailt Macnamara, daughter of the Chief of Clann Cuilein. Their son Murrough, Prince of Thomond, made his submission to Henry VIII in 1542. In the next year Murrough, whom the Lord Deputy described as 'a man of such sobriety and towardness that there is good hope of him', crossed to England and resigned into the King's hands his captainship, title, superiority and country, and was created Earl of Thomond in recompense.

Donogh, fourth Earl of Thomond, known as the 'Great Earl', fought with the English against the Irish, and was rewarded with a pension for life of £200 per annum by Queen Elizabeth in 1589. When he succeeded to the earldom in 1581 he chose to live at Bunratty.

The castle is a great rectangular edifice with square towers projecting at each corner, the southern and northern ones joined by a distinctive high, wide arch rising to below the top storey. The Earl made many improvements. He added to the top storeys of the towers, covered the roof of the castle with lead, inserted stained glass in some of the windows,

embellished the interior with the chimney-piece in the main guard, and had fine elaborate scroll and floral stucco-work applied to walls and ceilings. Pieces of this stucco decoration survive in the chapel in the south-east tower, just off the great hall, where it includes emblems of the Holy Eucharist, and also in the great hall itself. This impressive chamber, where the Earl held court and received formally, rose to a height of 48 feet, was 48 feet long and 30 feet wide, with a paved marble floor. It had neither fireplace nor chimney; it was heated by a brazier in the centre of the room, and the smoke escaped through a louvre in the roof. The present timber roof is a replacement by the Board of Public Works, modelled on the surviving medieval roof of Dunsoghly Castle, Co. Dublin. The general eating-room of the castle was the main guard below the great hall, where undoubtedly the soldiery spent much of their time and slept. It has a minstrels' gallery. The Earl's private apartments, the solar which commanded a full view of the great hall through a hatch, the private chapel and the bedchamber are reached from the great hall by flights of stairs in the north-east and north-west towers.

Archbishop Rinuccini, the Papal Nuncio, who visited the sixth Earl of Thomond at Bunratty in 1646 during his mission to Ireland, was most impressed by the castle, the ponds, and the park with its three thousand head of deer. As Rinuccini must have seen many splendid and luxurious palaces in Italy, one assumes that it was the medieval grandeur of Bunratty and its unusual setting which impressed him, rather than the beauty of the architecture, furnishings or decoration.

In the Civil War the sixth Earl declared for Parliament, surrendered his castle and went to live in England, whereupon the Confederates besieged the Commonwealth commander Admiral Penn to whom it had been surrendered. This Admiral Penn was the father of William Penn, the founder of Pennsylvania, who therefore will have passed some of his boyhood at Bunratty. Eventually the property was acquired by a settler family, the Studderts, who lived in a house adjoining the castle walls until they built a Georgian mansion in the demesne.

The castle fell into disrepair, but it has now been superbly and sensitively repaired and restored by the Office of Public Works, with financial assistance from Lord Gort, who had acquired it in 1956, and Bord Failte, the Irish Tourist Board. It now houses a magnificent collection of medieval furniture, vessels, paintings, sculpture and tapestries – French, Flemish, German, Spanish and English. The table in the solar, loaned by Lord Inchiquin, has long been in his branch of the O'Brien family; it is said to have come from Leamaneh Castle and to have been made of pieces salvaged from a wrecked Armada ship. Most of the other beautiful furnishings were the collection of Lord Gort. Due to his munificence the buildings and its contents are now held in trust for the Irish nation.

The great hall, the audience-chamber of the Earls of Thomond

Burncourt Castle CO. TIPPERARY

'Fifteen days it was burning' – the shell of the strong-house

The name of this seventeenth-century strong-house, frequently spelt 'Burntcourt', is a translation of the Irish name *Cuirt-doigte* by which it was known locally after it was burned in 1650. The original name of the place was Clogheen; it is referred to rather quaintly as 'Burnt-Clogheen' in an inquisition of 1693.

The castle was built by Sir Richard Everard, the first Baronet, on lands granted to him by Charles I, and erected into the 'Manor of Everard's Castle' by Letters Patent of 1639. According to an old jingle long remembered in the area, the castle was 'seven years in building, seven years living in it and fifteen days it was burning'. Its date-stone with the date 1641 is now inserted in a wall near the entrance to the farmyard which is adjacent to the ruin.

During the Civil War Sir Richard, a Catholic Royalist and a prominent member of the Kilkenny Confederation, managed to defeat a Parliamentary force. Cromwell, incensed, retaliated by attacking Everard's Castle in 1650. It was burned, according to some, by the Parliamentarians; according to others by Lady Everard who set fire to her house to prevent its use by the enemy. Sir Richard was subsequently taken and hanged.

The scheme of Burncourt is similar to that of Kanturk, with four attached flanking towers projecting from the corners of a central rectangle. There was a timber guard-walk over the front door supported by stone corbels, as well as numerous firing holes, but the many gables and rows of mullioned windows give the castle a peaceful, residential appearance.

61

Cahir Castle CO. TIPPERARY

A superbly defensive castle, considered impregnable until the advent of heavy cannon. Its garrison surrendered to Cromwell's letter of threat, written 'before Cahir', without a fight. Above, *detail of the first gate into the inner ward with portcullis, and* right, *the walls rising from the River Suir*

The name Cahir, deriving from the Irish *cathair,* or 'stone fort', suggests that the present site of the castle on a rock-islet in a bend of the River Suir was once the site of an Iron Age ring-fort. The destruction of a fort there about the third century is mentioned in the *Book of Lecan.* Indeed it is likely that a series of forts were erected on the spot through the centuries, though the Anglo-Norman invaders neglected it when they advanced westwards against Domhnall Mor O'Brien, King of Thomond, in 1192, choosing rather to build a great motte elsewhere on the Suir, at Knockgraffon. The barony of Cahir was granted to Philip of Worcester in 1215, who was succeeded by his nephew William; eventually it passed to the de Berminghams through the marriage of the Worcester heiress, Basilia, to Milo de Bermingham. When William de Bermingham was attained and executed in 1332 the lands were forfeited to the Crown. It appears that these Hiberno-Norman lords all used Knockgraffon, the *caput baroniae,* as their seat.

James Butler, third Earl of Ormond, was enfeoffed of the manor of Cahir in 1375, and at his death in 1405 he was succeeded in that part of his vast possessions by one of his natural sons, James, the issue of his liaison with his mistress and niece Lady Katherine Fitzgerald, a daughter of the third Earl of Desmond. This son, Seamus Gallda (James the Foreigner), ancestor of the Butlers, Barons of Cahir, made Cahir his seat early in the fifteenth century. It was he who built the castle, the largest of that date in the country.

We can still gain from Cahir an excellent idea of a feudal courtyard-complex. The high enclosing walls are defended by eight towers, five round and three rectangular. Within the walls are three irregularly shaped courts or wards: outer, middle and inner. The spacious outer ward, almost a rectangle, enclosing about 16,800 square feet, was large enough to accommodate cattle and soldiery in times of attack. In the smaller middle ward there were no buildings; the inner ward, however, contains the massive keep, the central *donjon* of the Norman castle where the lord had his residence, dominating the whole compound. The great hall for audiences and banquets, built against the west wall with its three west windows overlooking the river, is a refinement added in the sixteenth century. A view of the castle in *Pacata Hibernia* in 1599 shows it to have looked then basically as it does today.

The Barons of Cahir occupied a vulnerable position between the borders of the powerful rival palatinates of the Butlers, Earls of Ormond and Fitzgeralds, Earls of Desmond, so it is not surprising that their castle was

made highly defensible. The barbican outside the east wall defended the entrance to the outer ward on the south side. The only access from the middle to the inner ward is through two gates between the keep and the east wall, the first of which is protected not only by a machicoulis above it, but also by a portcullis which could be raised and lowered. The parapet of the tower to the east also commanded this entrance. It was long considered that this series of defences was infallible. Reynolds, secretary to Devereux, Earl of Essex, described Cahir in 1599 as: 'the only famous castle in Ireland which was thought impregnable and is the bulwark for Munster, and a safe retreat for all the agents of Spain and Rome'. Essex, however, besieged the castle for several days, battering it with his modern artillery; its surrender was the only military success of significance during his otherwise disastrous campaign in Ireland.

In 1647 the castle was surrendered again, this time to that barbarous Parliamentarian Lord President of Munster, Murrogh O'Brien, Lord Inchiquin, whose

The first of two gates between the middle and inner wards, with flanking tower, machicoulis and portcullis

ruthless methods earned him the name 'Murrogh of the Burnings'.

In 1650 Cromwell himself was before Cahir Castle and demanded its surrender. The then Baron was a minor, so it was to his guardian Captain George Mathew that Cromwell sent a peremptory invitation to surrender, which has been preserved:

> Before Cahir, 24th February, 1650
>
> Sir – Having brought the army and my cannon near this place according to my usual manner in summoning places, I thought fit to offer you terms honourable to soldiers: that you may march away with your baggage, arms and colours, free from injuries or violence. But if I be, not withstanding, necessitated to bend my cannon upon you, you must expect the extremity usual in such cases. To avoid blood, this is offered to you by
>
> Your servant,
>
> Oliver Cromwell

Captain Mathew had undoubtedly heard what the 'extremity usual in such cases' would be, so his garrison surrendered and left with their banners, arms and baggage. The estate was confiscated and surveyed by Petty, but it was never actually allotted to Cromwellians, so that it was not difficult at the Restoration for the Viceroy, Ormond, to manoeuvre the reinstatement of his kinsman, the Baron of Cahir, by a letter of the King dated 22 September 1662.

This cadet branch of the house of Ormond remained staunchly Catholic; the seventh Baron fought for James II at Aughrim and was outlawed, but subsequently the attainder was reversed and his estates including the castle were restored to him. His successors, Catholics and Jacobites, found it wiser to live abroad, where they distinguished themselves with the Irish brigades on the Continent and in foreign service. On the death without issue of the eleventh Baron in 1788 the title was claimed by a distant kinsman, Richard Butler of Glengall, who later became Earl of Glengall. As the senior branch had lived abroad and this junior branch had another residence, no attempt was made to convert the castle. This accounts for the buildings' practically unchanged appearance. Some necessary repairs were effected in 1840, and the hall was converted for use for religious services. When the Glengall title became extinct on the death of the second Earl without male issue, the property passed to his daughter Lady Margaret Charteris and her descendants. The castle was acquired by the Commissioners of Public Works in 1964 as a National Monument. It has been skilfully restored and opened to the public.

Carrickfergus Castle CO. ANTRIM

Carrickfergus, standing in a commanding position on a rocky dyke jutting off the north shore of Belfast Lough, is the most complete early medieval castle in Ireland. It was begun in the 1180s by the Anglo-Norman adventurer John de Courcy, who built the inner ward at the seaward end of the promontory. De Courcy was defeated at Carrickfergus in 1204 by another adventurer, Hugh de Lacy, Earl of Ulster, who thus became possessed of the castle site. It was probably at this time that work was begun on the great square keep, an unbuttressed four-storey tower, 55 feet by 60 feet, and 90 feet high, with a main chamber 40 feet by 38 feet. At the same time, or soon after, the curtain wall of the middle ward was built, with a postern gate on the seaward side and projecting wall-towers strategically placed to allow covering arrow-fire. The keep would have taken about a decade to build, so that it was probably still not completed when King John, anxious to curb the autonomy of the Earl of Ulster, besieged Carrickfergus and took it in 1210. The arrangement of the walled ward with projecting towers is similar to the castle of another of the King's over-mighty subjects, Roger Bigod, Earl of Norfolk, whose keepless castle of Framlingham in England had been rebuilt between 1189 and 1213.

When Carrickfergus passed to the Crown, constables were appointed to command it. In 1214 a sum was allotted for work on the 'great tower and a small turret' as well as on a hall and a new granary. The hall was evidently built against the east wall of the inner ward, at first-floor level over an undercroft; its windows with window-seats survive. We can observe the progress of construction in the materials used: in the earliest work purplish-brown and reddish-brown sandstone was used for the dressings; later creamy-yellow magnesian limestone was brought from Cultra, Co. Down, for the quoins at the angles of the keep and for the dressings on the wall-towers. The builders achieved a fine effect with the contrast of light sandstone and black basalt.

The gate-house has flanking circular drum-towers spanned by a high machicolation arch which carried a timber platform for the defence of the entrance, and its style points to a building date about 1250. The curtain wall of the outer ward was built at the same time.

Edward Bruce attacked the castle when he invaded Ireland in 1315. It fell to his brother King Robert Bruce, after a siege which lasted over a year, in the course of which, it is reported, the beleaguered garrison survived by eating eight of the Scots prisoners who had died there. The inner and outer portcullis of the entrance passage and its segmented

The curtain wall rising from a basalt dyke on the shore of Belfast Lough

vault were inserted early in the fourteenth century, probably when the Crown recaptured the castle after the defeat of the Bruces, but by 1390 the castle was reported to be 'totally destitute and desolate of defence'.

A number of repairs and improvements were carried out in the latter half of the sixteenth century. Sir Henry Sidney had the keep reroofed, the store-houses against the north-east wall of the outer ward were built, and the walls and parapets were modified so that guns could be swivelled to command a wide view from externally splayed gunports and embrasures. In 1591 the ditch which cut the narrow tongue of rock on the landward side was filled in, and a masonry arch was inserted in the great main chamber of the keep. Despite these works, in 1605 the Lord Deputy reported that the castle was 'much needing repair'. In 1642 General Monroe with a large force of Scots auxiliaries took the castle; subsequently the Parliamentarian General Monk surprised the garrison and captured the castle. His term as governor was short. The next year Lord Inchiquin captured the castle for the King, only to lose it a few months later to Sir Charles Coote, who was appointed governor for the Commonwealth.

In 1690 General Schomberg besieged Carrickfergus and took it for King William III, who landed in Ireland under its walls on 14 June. The next reigning monarch to visit the castle was Queen Elizabeth II, who landed at Carrickfergus from the Royal yacht on her visit to Northern Ireland in the summer of 1961.

After many years of use as an armoury and magazine the castle was transferred to the Northern Ireland Government in 1928 to be preserved as a National Monument. It now houses a military museum.

A royal castle, looking today much as it did when it was built in the twelfth to thirteenth centuries

Carrickkildavnet Castle CO. MAYO

Despite the lack of interior light, bleak aspect and isolated situation, tower-houses such as this were inhabited by entire families and their retainers

This small fifteenth-century castle was probably built by the O'Malleys, and tradition associates the pirate queen Grace O'Malley with the place (p. 190). It stands beside an inlet of the sea and had a boat-slip, fragments of which remain. The castle is now preserved as a National Monument.

Carrick-on-Suir Castle CO. TIPPERARY

In the reign of Elizabeth I (who was his kinswoman through the Boleyns), the tenth Earl of Ormond built a spacious mansion of completely English appearance on to the fifteenth-century castle of his forebears. Two ruined towers survive of the old castle, which was built around a square ward on the bank of the River Suir. The Elizabethan house occupies the north side of the cobbled courtyard, enclosing the east and west.

The style of this mansion, unique in Ireland at least among surviving buildings, was dictated by the personal taste of the Anglophile Earl who spent many years at the English court. The Virgin Queen, a year his junior, is said to have called the dark, amorous Irishman, 'my black husband'. Indeed there is a persistent rumour that at the age of twenty she bore him a son: one of his many natural children, Piers Butler of Duiske, conceived in the autumn of 1553. However this may be, throughout his long life 'Black Tom' remained steadfastly devoted to the Queen, and cherished the hope that she would one day be his guest at Carrick, where he decorated the great hall with stucco medallions of her crowned head between figures representing Justice and Equity. His and her portraits in stucco also decorate the entrance passage.

Altogether the Earl's mansion was a gracious and comfortable place, quite alien to contemporary buildings and usages in Ireland. It is a long, low building, two storeys high with attics, lit by rows of mullioned windows with those round-headed lights with hood-mouldings which were then fashionable in England. The brick gables are crowned by slender column-like finials. The long gallery or hall which runs the full length of the first floor on the front is a delightful room whose counterpart can be found in Tudor and Jacobean England, though not in Ireland, with a finely decorated stucco ceiling and wall panels. There were two fireplaces with brick chimneys and ornate stone chimney-pieces. The Earls hung there fine tapestries, both from the Continent and from the manufactory founded in Kilkenny with Flemish artisans by the eighth Earl.

The firing holes above and beside the round-headed front door are a reminder that the house was liable to attack. Its non-fortified character was only made possible by the old castle which served to protect it. It is clear that both buildings were used as one unit, despite their great dissimilarity, for the hearth tax of 1663 lists Carrick Castle with thirty hearths. A considerable part of the old castle was destroyed in the Civil War by Cromwell.

The residential character of the mansion ensured its continued occupation even after the family chose to live in Kilkenny Castle. In 1695 it was rented to a Captain James Johnson. In 1816 the tenant Mr Wogan carried out some essential repairs, but subsequently the house fell into decay, although in 1840 some valuable tapestries still hung there.

The whole complex is now a National Monument. The mansion has been skilfully repaired and restored.

The towers of the fifteenth-century Ormond castle appear behind the neat gables of an Elizabethan English-style manor house

Carrigafoyle Castle CO. KERRY

Above *and* right, *views inside the ruined five-storey tower. The stone quoins once carried the wooden floors. See Colour Plate III*

The remarkable stronghold of the O'Connors of Kerry was built about the end of the fifteenth or beginning of the sixteenth century on the estuary of the River Shannon. Its name in Irish means 'rock of the chasm'. It was defended on the landward side by the two curtain walls, both fortified, the inner one with rounded turrets, the outer with square towers at the corners. In the bawn, which was open towards the water, was a dock, so that boats could sail right up to the castle. This unique and useful arrangement was made possible by the siting of the castle between the high- and low-water marks, so that at low tide it is accessible from the road across a path of stones to the outer bawn wall, while at high tide this path was submerged and the castle became an island, as it still does at very high tides.

The five-storey tower rises to a height of 80 feet and is beautifully constructed, with courses of carefully selected small stones, neatly laid. The second and fourth storeys of the tower are covered by vaults. A breach in the wall of the tower on the landward side has revealed the section of the building, so that the steep-pointed vault of the fourth floor can be seen, as well as the small chambers constructed in the haunches of the vault to help carry the great weight.

A plan of the castle drawn in pen and ink in April 1580 has been preserved among the State Papers in the Public Records Office, London. It was enclosed in a letter sent to Queen Elizabeth by her Deputy in Ireland, Sir William Pelham, in the year he besieged a mixed garrison of Irish, Italians and Spaniards at Carrigafoyle, part of the expeditionary force sent to back the rebellion in Ireland. Pelham wrote to the Queen: 'If God give us bread we doubt not but to make as bare a country as ever a Spaniard set his foot in.' His modern cannon destroyed a part of the building, so he was able to take Carrigafoyle, and the garrison to a man was put to the sword.

The O'Connor Kerry later recaptured the castle, only to surrender it again in 1600 when it was attacked by the Lord Deputy, Sir George Carew, after which it was granted by the Crown to Sir Charles Wilmot. In 1659 the titulados were John Edmond and John Hill.

Despite its damaged condition and inconvenient situation the castle was still inhabited in the last century by a Dr Edward Fitzmaurice and his family; his father-in-law, Dr William Odell, Deputy Inspector of Hospitals in Ireland, died there in 1865. It is now a National Monument.

Castle Balfour CO. FERMANAGH

Castle Balfour, built in 1618 by Sir James Balfour from Fifeshire, Scotland, is a strong-house similar to Scottish buildings of the period. It was arranged on a T-plan, with a corbelled-out turret built at the angle of the main block and the west wing to contain a mural stair which rose from the main apartments on the first floor to the upper storeys. The kitchen and offices were on the vaulted ground floor, from which the first floor was reached by a timber stair. From the outside the front door would have been reached quite simply by a wooden ladder.

The parish church was built close to the castle, and the populous village of Lisnaskea grew up round it. The castle was refortified by Ludlow during the Civil War, but suffered in the troubles of 1689 when Lisnaskea was burnt. Nevertheless it was inhabited by a series of tenants into the last century. It is now in State care, having been handed over for that purpose by the Earl of Erne in 1960.

Left, the castle-mansion of a Scot dating from the Plantation of Ulster

Castle Bernard CO. CORK

Francis Bernard, an English settler who came to Ireland with the Plantation of Munster, or perhaps Francis his son, acquired the manor of Castle Mahon sometime after 1611 and before 1641, at which time the younger Francis held it. The manor and castle had been forfeited by its original owners, the O'Mahonys, for their part in the Desmond Rebellion in which Conoher O'Mahony of Castle Mahon was slain. In 1588 the property had been granted to a settler, Phane Beecher, who fled during the rising of 1598 but returned and had his grant confirmed in 1611.

After the Civil War Francis Bernard junior re-modelled the medieval castle the family had acquired by inserting large windows in the place of the slits and throwing down the bawn wall. This proved to be an unfortunate alteration, for he was killed when the castle was attacked by a party of Jacobites under Colonel M'Carthy in 1690. Bernard had gathered his family, retainers, and farmers into the castle and hoisted a red flag on the tower. In the ensuing attack many of the garrison lost their lives.

This Francis Bernard's son, another Francis, remembered as 'Judge Bernard', rebuilt the castle, adding a new, fashionable brick front on the River Bandon side, and changed its name to Castle Bernard. His son, yet another Francis, 'Squire Bernard', added

The ruined façade of the castle which was burned in the twentieth-century troubles

an eastern front in 1731 and laid out the park and beech avenue. During his occupancy a little Bernard child lost his balance while trying to swat bats in the tower with his battledore and fell to his death. In 1788 another Francis Bernard, who became first Earl of Bandon, pulled down the fronts which had been added and erected a new mansion 90 feet to the east of the old building, to which it was connected by a corridor.

During the spate of country-house burning in the troubles which preceded Irish independence, the fourth Earl and his wife were woken one night to be told that men had come to set fire to Castle Bernard. They dressed and went out pathetically into the park where they watched the castle and its contents, including a fine library, perish in the flames. The doughty Countess, a formidable *grande dame*, stood erect and tearless beside her husband and, it is said, defiantly sang *God Save the King*. The castle's shell is now a picturesque ivy-clad ruin, and the present Earl lives in a modern house near by.

Castle Garde CO. LIMERICK

Little is known of the history of attractive Castle Garde, which was inherited by Mr Hugh Thompson, the present owner, from the Guillamore O'Gradys. It was one of the many late-medieval fortresses of the Earls of Desmond, and appears to have changed hands many times since the confiscation of their palatinate. In the Civil Survey of 1654, Henry, Earl of Bath, is shown as the proprietor of 'Kass Lanengard', and in 1659 the titulados are listed as 'Henry Bally and his son John Bally gentlemen' at 'Castle ne Gaurde'. This would be the John Baylee ancestor of the Baylees of Lough Gur, who, according to the traveller Dineley, held Lough Gur Castle from the Dowager Countess of Bath in the reign of Charles II.

By 1837 Castle Garde, then more usually written Castle Guard, was in the possession of the Honourable Waller O'Grady, an ancestor of the present owner. The topographer Samuel Lewis described it then as 'an ancient castle of the Earls of Desmond enlarged and restored in the baronial style with a lofty keep and ramparts'. The restoration and additions which had been carried out in the 1820s, probably at the time of Mr O'Grady's marriage to the Honourable Grace Massy in 1823, are most skilful. The work has been attributed to James Pain, one of the architect brothers brought to Ireland and trained by Nash. The standard of the work, and the appearance of the castellated gate-lodge in the form of a circular tower, are entirely in keeping with this attribution. A two-storey castellated house with a Gothick façade was added to one side of the Desmond tower-house, whose windows were modified and enlarged so that the tower rooms could be conveniently used with those of the communicating addition.

The origin of the unusual stone effigies of Bacchus, Mars, and a goddess entwined with a fish, which are set on the inner side of the gateway, is obscure.

A medieval Geraldine tower-house with Gothick additions. Below, the gate-house from inside the bawn, with its curious mythological figures

V Glenveagh Castle CO. DONEGAL

The cod ramparts of a splendid Victorian castle, built on the edge of Lough Veagh. *See* p. 120.

VI Dunluce Castle CO. ANTRIM

The magnificent, brooding ruins of the castle perched on a rocky promontory high above the Atlantic breakers. Here Sorley Boy McDonnell mounted cannon salvaged from a wrecked Armada galleass. *See* p. 108.

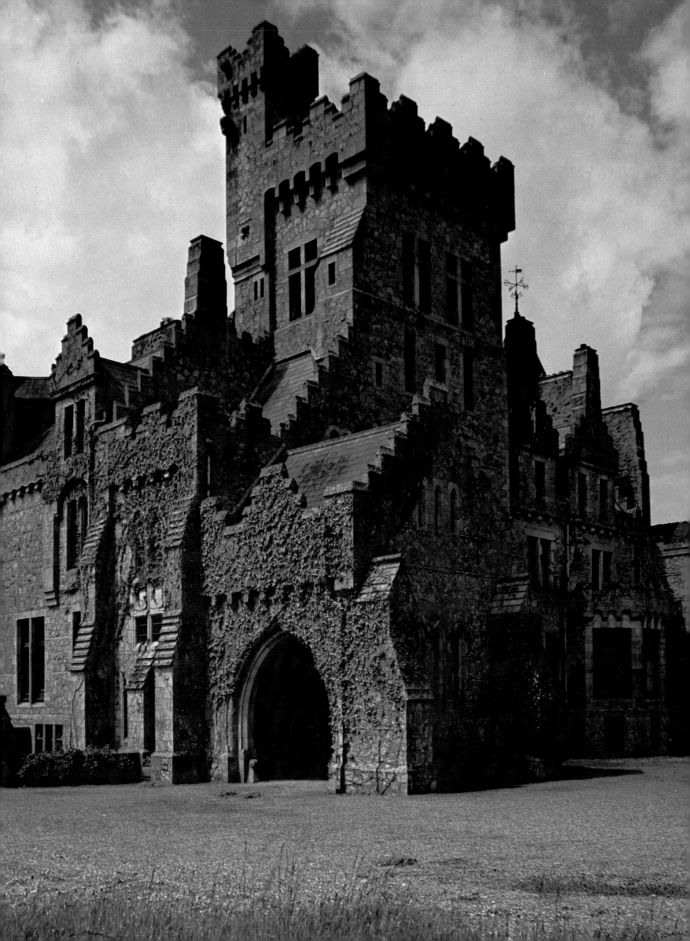

VII Humewood Castle CO. WICKLOW

Humewood was designed by the brilliant Victorian architect William White. *See* p. 140.

Castle Matrix CO. LIMERICK

Prominent on the banks of the River Deel, this tall keep commands views over the surrounding countryside to the Shannon and as far as the mountains of Tipperary and Clare.

The square tower, 80 feet high, with castellated bartizans rising another 10 feet from the angles of the parapet, was built about the middle of the fifteenth century by the Earls of Desmond. The Earls were then at the zenith of their power in Munster, and asserted their autonomy by erecting castles in strategic positions in their palatinate.

In 1580 the Earl of Desmond was in rebellion and had lost Castle Matrix to the forces of the Crown. The castle was repaired by Sir Walter Ralegh after he had successfully surprised an ambush of Irish rebels near by.

Once the rebellion was quelled the Desmond lands were confiscated and distributed to English planters. In the reign of James I Castle Matrix was in the possession of Edmond Southwell, one of three brothers from Suffolk who sought their fortune in the Irish colony, of whom John obtained Rathkeale Castle, renamed Castle Southwell, Richard, who was later knighted, was granted a licence in 1616 to keep forty taverns and to sell wine and acqua vitae in Limerick city, and Edmond took up residence at Castle Matrix, and is credited with being one of the first landowners in Ireland to cultivate the potato tubers imported from Virginia by Ralegh. He was in the castle in 1641 at the time of the insurrection when it was blockaded by the Irish, who built forts around it and eventually succeeded in taking it. It was recaptured little-damaged by Cromwell's troops, and in the Civil Survey of 1654 Edmond Southwell is shown as the proprietor of the lands, having on them 'a castle an orchard a grist mill and a tucking mill'. Edmond must have lived to a great age, for he is still shown as the titulado of 'Castle Matrickes', together with his son Thomas, in 1659. There were then six English, presumably members of his family, and twenty Irish living on the townland. The son Thomas served as Sheriff of Limerick, Kerry and Clare, was knighted as 'Sir Thomas Southwell of Castle Mattress' and created a Baronet of Ireland in 1662; his grandson, another Sir Thomas, was raised to the peerage as Baron Southwell of Castle Mattress in 1717, and his grandson the third Baron became the first Viscount Southwell in 1776.

The enjoyment of the castle went to the Brown family through the marriage of Meliora Southwell (a grand-daughter of the first Baron) to John Brown of Mount Brown in 1751. Their grandson, John Southwell Brown, decided in the 1830s to make the old castle his residence. The estate was then producing a good income thanks to the flour mill propelled by the current of the River Deel; fitted up with the newest machinery it was producing 20,000 barrels annually and employed one hundred persons, mostly the industrious descendants of German Protestant refugees whom the first Baron had welcomed to his estates in 1709.

The castle has now been given a new lease of life. Repaired and furnished with antiques it became in 1970 the home of the Irish International Arts Centre under the directorship of Mr Sean O'Driscoll.

A medieval tower with improvements made in the nineteenth century – mullioned windows, a castellated wing and parapets

Castle Oliver CO. LIMERICK

Also known by the townland name of 'Cloghanodfoy', the present nineteenth-century castle occupies the site of several older buildings. In 1654 Sir Edward Fitzharrys, Baronet, was shown in the Civil Survey as the proprietor of 'Cloghnotfoy' on which there was 'An old Ruyned stone house, A Bawne, stable, orchard and Garden'. In 1659 the titulado was Robert Oliver, a Cromwellian captain who had a confirmation of the grant under the Act of Settlement of 1666. It seems that he repaired the 'ruyned stone house' as a residence. In a drawing in the Down Survey of 1655 it appears as a rectangular bawn with a crenelated wall and four turrets with conical roofs at the angles. This was quite unlike any of the smaller Munster castles in plan.

The senior male branch of the Olivers continued at Cloghanodfoy, to which they gave their own name according to the prevailing fashion, until Richard Oliver of Castle Oliver changed his surname to Gascoigne on inheriting with his wife the estates of her step-father Sir Thomas Gascoigne at Parlington in Yorkshire in 1812. Thereupon the Gascoignes went to live in Yorkshire, and in 1837 Castle Oliver was reported to be in ruins. In due course the Irish and English estates were inherited by Gascoigne's daugh-

Above, the impressive pile built by an English architect immediately after the Famine, and right, a detail of the robust and individual design

ters Mary Isabella and Elizabeth, and in 1850, when the elder sister married, they decided that an additional residence would not be amiss. A York architect, G. Fowler Jones, was employed to design and build a baronial castle of dark reddish sandstone, complete with battered walls, stepped gables, turret-bartizans projecting on corbels from the corners and a fortified porte-cochère. The design is both studied and robust; the workmanship is of a good standard outside. The interior is stark and severe, though charmingly alleviated by an unusual chimney-piece with a glass surround painted by the Gascoigne sisters. They also painted a romantic window in the entrance hall depicting the life and miracles of St Patrick. The stable-block of the older Castle Oliver was preserved and survives. The present owner, who battles courageously to preserve this mammoth residence, is the great-grand-daughter of the elder sister Mary Isabella and her husband Frederick Charles Trench, who assumed her surname of Gascoigne in addition to his own.

Clonmines CO. WEXFORD

A ruin of a fortified church in the abandoned medieval town,
above, *and* right, *the 'Town Hall', one of its castles*

A thriving walled town in medieval times, with a number of castles and a harbour, Clonmines lost its importance at the end of the sixteenth century when the silver and lead mines which had been the source of its prosperity became worked out. The population dwindled, and by the seventeenth century, when the port had silted up, the town was practically deserted. Much of the town had been damaged when it was attacked in 1400, so that most of the surviving ruins of this medieval ghost-town are of buildings constructed shortly after that date, with a strong encircling wall and town gates of which vestiges remain.

The two-storey castellated building known as the 'Town Hall' served as the council chamber of the town and was also used by the ecclesiastical court. It may also have housed the treasury and muniments. The galleried ground floor is unusual: one half of the ceiling is vaulted with ribbed arches, the other half is a barrel vault. It has two entrance doorways.

Ruins of some churches and residential tower-houses within the walls also survive. Of particular interest is the fortified nave-and-chancel church with its battlemented tower at the west end. This was built early in the fifteenth century, at about the time fortified churches with towers were being built in other parts of Ireland. Another notable example survives at Taghmon, Co. Westmeath. At Dunsany and at Killeen in Co. Meath the fifteenth-century churches were fortified with not one but two protecting towers. These thick-walled towers provided not only a residence for the clergy, but also a sacristy and a treasury. As long as the Church's ancient privilege of sanctuary was observed, influential laymen took advantage of it to store their precious metals and jewels as well as food-supplies such as malt and bacon. At the dissolution of the monasteries in Ireland the friary and property of the Augustinians at Clonmines was granted to Laurence Nevill, and they were formally expelled. The lonely seclusion of Clonmines, however, enabled them to remain there surreptitiously, and even during the Penal times a few of them continued to live with singular persistence near the ruins of their former friary, until in 1773 a chapel was built for them at Grantstown Farm.

Until 1800, Clonmines as an ancient borough continued to return a member to the Irish Parliament, although for over a century it had been a constituency practically without electors.

This interesting medieval site has never been excavated. It is now a National Monument, though somewhat neglected and subject to vandalism.

Clonony Castle CO. OFFALY

This sixteenth-century four-storey tower-house standing in a spacious bawn continued to be used as a residence into the nineteenth century, when it was renovated and the internal walls were plastered. At that time, too, the bawn wall and gateway were rebuilt.

The tower seen through the entrance arch of the bawn

Coolhull Castle CO. WEXFORD

Built towards the end of the sixteenth century, the unique castle at Coolhull departed from the usual tower-house type then fashionable. It is a long, rectangular building only two storeys high, with remarkable crenellations. Above the roof at one end rises a small narrow tower; the other end has a protective bartizan projecting on corbels from one

A beautifully preserved miniature castle with crenellations, a rectangular block and a single tower

corner. The round-headed windows of the upper storey give the building a residential air, while the unusual plan allowed for spacious chambers and a comfortable disposition of rooms for domestic use.

Creagh Castle CO. GALWAY

The *Composicion Book of Conaght* compiled in 1574 contains a list of the castles in the county of Galway: there were then no fewer than two hundred and seventy. Some were built by the old Gaelic chiefs, like the O'Flahertys or O'Shaughnessys. The greater number were built by the Connaught landowners of Norman descent who had become hibernicized after four centuries in this outlying region. The most powerful of these landowners were the Burkes who possessed about fifty castles, mostly tower-houses erected in the fifteenth and sixteenth centuries, of which Creagh Castle on the road from Loughrea to Ardrahan is typical.

At the turn of the century Creagh housed a still for making the unlicensed whisky, poteen, for which the mountainous areas of the county were once famous. Secret distillers in the castle found the look-out posts at the top of its tower still serviceable for keeping watch for raids by the Royal Irish Constabulary.

One of the innumerable tower-houses which pepper the Connaught landscape

Doe Castle CO. DONEGAL

Doe Castle, once better known as Castledoe, was the stronghold of the MacSweeny Doe (MacSuibhne na dTuath), from whom it derives its name. The site is a low, rocky peninsula which juts out into Sheephaven Bay, admirably suited for defence; the castle is surrounded by the sea on three sides, while on the landward side the entrance is by a little bridge over a moat which was created by hewing a fosse out of the rock.

A sturdy, four-storey, sixteenth-century central keep, rising to a height of 55 feet, still dominates the compound, though it is much altered internally and hemmed in by later constructions. It stands within a rectangular turretted and battlemented bawn.

The MacSweenys, fiery, quarrelsome and quick to anger, were originally mercenaries in the service of the O'Donnells and acquired a considerable territory in Donegal as their payment. The first mention of their castle is in 1544, when the sons of the MacSweeny Doe were embroiled in a fratricidal conflict. The victor was eventually slain, as was one of his sons who succeeded him as chief. Thereafter for many years the ownership of the castle was fought over and disputed incessantly.

Owen (Eoghan Oge) who succeeded his brother in the chieftancy was one of the few chatelains to die naturally. A patron of the bards, who extolled his hospitality, he harboured shipwrecked sailors of the Spanish Armada in his castle, as well as the O'Rorke of Breffny who was on the run from the authorities. The next chief, his nephew, best remembered as Sir Miles MacSweeny, sided with the English and gained as a reward a knighthood, a grant of the estate by Royal patent and a pension. He was ousted by Red Hugh O'Donnell from Castledoe where, it is said, he had brained disobedient vassals in the great hall. To placate Red Hugh, Sir Miles deserted the English cause, thereby contriving to enjoy a joint tenure of the estate with his cousin, Owen the younger (Eoghan Oge), who was Red Hugh's foster-brother. This Owen espoused the English cause and was besieged in the castle by Red Hugh and Sir Miles in alliance. Having held the castle with help from the English, Owen changed allegiance for the last time when its custody was given by Royal warrant to Red Hugh's brother and successor, Rory O'Donnell, Earl of Tyrconnell. Owen was executed by the English at Lifford in 1605, but this was by no means the end of the struggle for possession of Castledoe. During Earl Rory's absence the castle was taken by Owen's brother Niall MacSweeny and others, who were expelled and punished when the Earl returned. The Government then compelled the Earl to allow Sir Basil Brooke to occupy Castledoe and its lands. The Earl of Tyrconnell sailed for the Continent from Lough Swilly in 1607, never to return, and Castledoe was once again in Crown hands. But it was shortly seized by the rebels of Sir Cahir O'Doherty, who slew all but one of the six warders stationed there. The Anglo-Irish force which recaptured the castle included its one-time owner, Sir

The view over Sheephaven Bay from the ramparts

Miles MacSweeny, who had once more changed his allegiance.

Under the Plantation of Ulster the lands of Castledoe were granted in 1611 to Sir Richard Bingley with a proviso that he maintain the castle, which was not, however, included in the grant. It was granted with its curtilage in 1614 to the Attorney-General, Sir John Davys, who sold it almost immediately to a Captain John Sandford. Sandford purchased also the lands held by Bingley, and Pynnar, who made his survey in 1619, reported: 'Captain Sanford hath 500 acres called Castledoe. Upon this there is a Bawn of Lyme and Stone forty feet square, sixteen feet high and a Castle

within it that is very strong; himself with his Wife and Family dwelling therein, with four other English Families on the Land.'

In the Rising of 1641 the castle was taken from Sandford's Irish son-in-law by the Confederates, and held for them by a descendant of the original owners, Captain Donnell MacSweeny, son of Niall. Sir Phelim O'Neill and other Northern leaders were at Castledoe to welcome Owen Roe O'Neill, who landed there by boat from Spain with one hundred followers. The Parliamentarians did not capture the castle until 1650.

For some years after the Civil War the Government, realizing the importance of the stronghold, main-

ownership as derived from the Sandford grant uncertain. George Vaughan eventually purchased the estate in 1759, and his grandson General George Vaughan Harte bought out the other heirs at the end of the century and set about the repair of the castle, adding a residence to the keep. After repairing the bawn he placed cannon captured at Seringapatam on gun carriages on the seaward terrace, and on the turrets. His son Captain John Harte, who succeeded to the property in 1832, befriended a poor itinerant tinsmith named Eamon MacSwyne, and provided work for him at the castle. This Eamon was a direct descendant of the chieftains, and apparently a grandson or great-grandson of the castle's last occupier, the Jacobite Donogh Oge MacSweeny.

After the Hartes left Doe Castle in the 1840s a number of tenants lived there, but from the 1890s it was left uninhabited and uncared-for. In the fervour of the Celtic Revival a *Feis* – a Gaelic festival – was held at Doe Castle in 1905, attended by thousands of people who marched from Creeslough down the ancient road to the castle. At their head, piping the 'McSwyne's March', was a Donegal piper who had won international acclaim at the Chicago World Fair in 1896. His name was Turlogh MacSweeny, and he claimed to be the heir to Doe, the lineal descendant of the old chieftains.

A legend connected with the castle persists. Sir Miles MacSweeny, to prevent the marriage of his daughter Eileen to her lover Turlogh Oge O'Boyle, having intercepted the young man at a tryst with her, is said to have imprisoned him and starved him to death. Eileen, according to the tale, on seeing the corpse of her suitor from an upper window, jumped to her death from the top of the tower. Available facts belie the tradition, for Turlogh Oge O'Boyle of Faugher outlived Sir Miles MacSweeny of Doe by many years. The tragic fate of the lovers was immortalized in a delightful ballad composed in the last century by Niall MacGiolla Bhrighde, a Creeslough poet, and published by Standish O'Grady; and fishermen claim that by moonlight a phantom skiff may often be seen crossing the bay, bearing the smiling ghosts of Turlogh Oge and Eileen.

In 1923 the Land Commission purchased the ruined castle, which became a National Monument.

tained it as a military garrison, spending a substantial sum on its repair and munitions. The MacSweenys were still about: Sir Miles's grandson Colonel Miles MacSweeny had so coveted his ancestral home during the Civil War that it was reported that he would have changed sides if allowed to enjoy it as a knight or squire. In 1689, when the Williamite garrison fled to Derry before the oncoming army of James II, Donogh Oge MacSweeny, grandson of Colonel Miles, seized Castledoe for the Jacobites and installed himself there.

When Bishop Pococke visited Doe on his tour in 1752 he noted its tall tower and encompassing walls. For many years it had then been uninhabited, its

---

Surrounded by water, Doe's position is both highly defensible and singularly poetic

Donegal Castle

The handsome fortified gabled house built on to the fifteenth-century tower

Captain Basil Brooke from Cheshire came to Ireland with the English Army in 1598. He fought in Munster, and in the conquest of Ulster was appointed a servitor of the Ulster Plantation and a Commissioner for the settlement of the Church of Ireland. In 1616 the King rewarded him for his services with a knighthood and a lease of lands in Donegal, formerly the territory of the O'Donnells of Tyrconnell. In 1623 Sir Basil received a permanent grant of the lands which included the borough of Donegal and the castle of the O'Donnell chiefs, built in the fifteenth century. He repaired the large, strong turreted tower which had been Hugh Roe O'Donnell's residence before he left to fight at Kinsale and sail to exile and death in Spain.

Brooke united to the tower a five-bay, three-storey gabled manor house in the English tradition which he built at right angles to it. To make the tower more agreeable and unite it architectonically with the house he added gables, and replaced the slit windows with

The view of the manor house from the massive tower built by the O'Donnells

three- and four-mullioned lights with hood-mouldings matching those of the new building. It is clear that the tower and the house were used as one residential unit, for the main chamber on the first floor of the tower has a grand and very ornate Jacobean chimney-piece, elaborately carved with the armorial escutcheons of Sir Basil and his wife, with swags, scrolls, chains and rosettes. Much less ornate, but elegant, is the round-headed doorway on the first-floor front of the house. The steps which must have given access to it have vanished. Both Sir Basil and his son and successor Sir Henry served as Governors of County Donegal. In Henry Brooke's time, during the Civil War when he sided with the Parliamentarians, Clanrickarde surprised and captured Donegal Castle, but he was only able to hold it for three days before it was recaptured. Basil, son of Sir Henry, the next chatelain, successfully defended the castle against the Jacobite forces under Sarsfield. It is now a National Monument.

The magnificent Jacobean chimney-piece, bearing the arms of Brooke impaling Leicester, and of Brooke, for the adventurer Sir Basil Brooke and his wife

Dromore Castle CO. LIMERICK

Edward William Godwin, the architect of Dromore Castle, was one of the most brilliant designers of the mid-Victorian period – intelligent, non-conformist, independent – though his unusual talents were often hampered by the limited vision or special exigencies of his clients. In the young third Earl of Limerick, however, he found a client-patron who not only allowed him a free rein, but encouraged him to employ his capacities to the utmost.

The Earl had succeeded at the age of twenty-six to Irish estates of over 5,700 acres in the counties of Cork and Limerick, and to the substantial annual income these yielded were added lucrative ground rents from buildings in Limerick city. For most of the nineteenth century the Earls of Limerick had lived in England as absentee landlords. They had no country seat in Ireland; during their visits they lived at Limerick House, an eighteenth-century town-house in the city. On succeeding to the title the third Earl resolved to build a splendid castle on his Irish lands. He was keenly interested in architecture, and as President of the Architectural Society in London, was closely associated with the Vice-President, Godwin. It was therefore to Godwin he entrusted the task of designing and building a castle on the superb site he had chosen a few miles from Limerick: an eminence overlooking the Shannon, and with a view of the romantic ancient stronghold of Carrigogunnell.

Dromore was not Godwin's first important commission, he had already successfully completed Town Halls at Northampton and Congleton in England, but it was a commission which offered him unique scope.

The dominating, wind-swept setting contributes to Dromore's romantic effect. Below, Godwin, *the architect, loved to contemplate the silhouette of his archaeological extravaganza by moonlight*

In collaboration with the enthusiastic Earl, eight years his junior, Godwin decided to eschew the Venetian-Gothic and French-Gothic Revival styles which then enjoyed great popularity in England, and with which he was familiar, in favour of a building of Irish inspiration. He travelled about Munster visiting and surveying medieval buildings, filling his sketchbooks with accurate designs not only of tower-houses and castles but also of ecclesiastical ruins. One source of inspiration in his design for Dromore was an ecclesiastical site, the group of buildings dramatically perched on the Rock of Cashel. At the same time he decided that Dromore should have not just the appearance but the reality of massive impregnability, with fortifications fit for a medieval stronghold. He justified this decision by pointing out the danger of attack by the Fenians, whose rising had then caused widespread alarm. The Earl did not demur, and the great walls of Dromore rose six feet thick with a battered base, like those of an authentic early fortress.

The *Building News* of 1867 endorsed Godwin's pretext for extravagance: 'The corridors are kept on the outer side of the building and all the entrances are well-guarded, so that in the event of the country being disturbed the inmates of Dromore Castle might not only feel secure themselves but be able to give real shelter to others.' As the Limericks were not popular landlords it is possible that his defences did comfort the aesthete Earl.

Hardly a feature of the medieval Irish castle repertory is missing: stepped crenellated parapets, machicolations supported by projecting corbels, slits, battlements, wall-walks, and a separate banqueting-hall. The whole of this fascinating complex is, however, marvellously integrated. Topped with a round-tower with a conical roof, the building was finished in two years. The interior was decorated by Godwin in the affected style dear to his mistress Ellen Terry and favoured by his avant-garde coterie in London. The ponderous Gothic arches and lofty rooms were hung with Japanese curtains. A determinedly Oriental flavour predominated, too, in the choice of porcelain, wall-paintings, potted plants and fabrics. Godwin himself designed much of the furniture. This was all apparently to the taste of the accommodating Earl.

The haste with which the building was completed, combined with Godwin's impracticality, resulted in an immediate problem with damp, which could never be eliminated. Godwin experienced the same problem with another Irish castle which he began in 1867: Glenbegh Towers situated above Dingle Bay in Co. Kerry. There the damp penetrated so extensively that he was sued by the owners. The Earl of Limerick was too delighted with the general result to cavil over inconveniences, but as the trouble worsened he spent less time at Dromore and more at his English seat, Tewin Water in Hertfordshire, where he died. After the First World War, and only fifty years after the castle was built, the Limericks abandoned Dromore; all in all they had hardly lived there.

The skyline was an important feature of the Victorian mansion and one of which Godwin was very conscious. Delighted with his achievement at Dromore, he sketched the wonderful silhouette by moonlight. The interior of the castle has now been dismantled, but the shell's vigorous towers still break the skyline to enchant us as Godwin intended.

The juxtaposition of assorted Irish and Gothic features is surprisingly successful

Dublin Castle

The medieval Record Tower flanked on one side by symmetrical eighteenth-century building and on the other by the Gothic Revival chapel

On 30 August 1204 King John signed an order to his half-brother Meiler FitzHenry, the Justiciar of Ireland, to build a fortress in Dublin. Though the principal purpose was to provide a place of safe-keeping for the Royal treasure, the King specified that the building should have strong walls and good ditches so that it could serve to defend the city if need be. Meiler was instructed to begin by erecting one tower, to which a castle and bailey could be added later, and he was empowered to choose a suitable site. The one he chose, which had most probably already served for a fortification of the Danish Kings of Dublin, and more recently of the Anglo-Norman invaders, was on a ridge above the marshy banks of the River Poddle (now an underground stream).

Construction continued under the Justiciar Henry de Loundres, who was also Archbishop of Dublin. Within a decade of the initial order the castle was substantially complete, with four towers guarding the curtain wall around a rectangular enclosure roughly corresponding with the present upper yard. The most important tower, Meiler FitzHenry's original building, stood at the north-east corner.

In 1228 payments were made for some work on the towers; three of these were drum-shaped, while the one at the south-west corner was smaller and rectangular. Within the walled bailey a chapel was built and its windows were glazed with stained glass in 1242. In 1243 an order was signed to build a detached hall. This was erected in the south-west part of the ward, roughly where St Patrick's Hall now stands, and consisted of a spacious chamber measuring 120 feet by 80 feet above a vaulted basement. The hall was rebuilt in 1320, and ten years later its windows were fitted with stained glass.

In the 1360s King Edward III sanctioned payments for building works by his son Lionel, Duke of Clarence, Viceroy of Ireland – improvements described by the King as 'divers work agreeable to him for Sports and his other pleasures as well in the Castle of Dublin and elsewhere'. Chivalrous tourneys, sports and games were then frequent and popular events in the castle. More towers were added to the four original ones, apparently also in the fourteenth century. A drum-tower, the 'Bermingham Tower', taller than all the others, was erected on the south wall adjacent to the rectangular corner tower, and a turret was built at the angle where the two lines of the south wall met. The gateway with a portcullis was on the north wall.

Comparatively little of these medieval buildings survives in the present castle. The most consequential and visible vestige is the south-east tower, once known as the 'Black Tower' and now called the 'Record Tower'. Even this narrowly escaped destruction when plans were afoot to pull it down at the end of the eighteenth century. Discussing the threatened demolition, the *Dublin Evening Post* of 3 September 1793 described the tower as 'the old black tower . . . a useless fabric that gives a disgraceful gloominess to the Viceregal residence, little according with the style and elegance of the other parts'. Its present machicolated parapet was added in 1819.

The battered base of the Bermingham Tower and about thirty yards of the old curtain wall to the south-east of it have also survived, but are hidden by later construction. The northern towers, one of which had been rebuilt in the seventeenth century, and one of the twin towers of the gate-house, which were also rebuilt in the seventeenth century, were pulled down about 1750 when most of the buildings now standing were built. The western tower of the gate-house was embedded in the new construction, in what is now the Genealogical Office, and supports the cupola-ed 'Bedford Tower'.

The medieval castle had never been a source of pride to the Viceroys after the Middle Ages. They found it shabby, unsuitable and ugly, despite desultory attempts to improve it, and their comments about it were invariably derogatory. In pursuance of Queen Elizabeth's command to make the castle 'a fit place for the reception of the chief governors', Sir Henry Sidney, then Lord Deputy, effected some repairs and embellishments, but by 1633 the Lord Deputy Wentworth reported: 'This Castle is in very great decay. I have been forced to take down one of the great Towers which was ready to fall and the rest are so crazy as we are still in fear part of it may drop upon our heads as one tower did whilst my Lord Chancellor was here. . . . There is not any stable but a poor mean one and that made out of a decayed church . . .' Summing up, he described his residential quarters as 'little better than a very prison'.

Only twenty years before the fire which destroyed much of the state and residential apartments and other buildings in 1684, the sum of £5,000 had been spent on general repairs. Nevertheless the Earl of Arran, who had been woken from sleep by the noise of the fire and the smoke, wrote of the disaster the next day to his father, the Viceroy Ormond: 'I find that the King has lost but six barrels of powder and the worst castle in the worst situation in Christiandom.' Lord Clarendon in letters to the Lord Treasurer two years later was equally scathing: 'It is the worst and most inconvenient lodging in the world,' he wrote, and 'never comes a shower of rain but it breaks into the house.'

Had Charles II not suffered from perennial financial problems, the city of Dublin might have had a handsome castle in the classical style, like Kilmainham Hospital which was then nearing completion. Instead the authorities decided to patch up the old fabric; the work was entrusted to the architect of Kilmainham, the Surveyor-General Sir William Robinson. A later Surveyor-General, Sir Edward Lovett Pearce, appointed to that office in 1730, decorated the ballroom of the castle for the then Viceroy, the Duke of Dorset. Mrs Delany who went to a ball there on a late autumn day

Below, a corridor and window in the Chapel Royal; right, an aisle. Francis Johnston's Gothic Revival work employs reiterated motifs to produce an almost musical effect

in 1731 was full of admiration for the effect Pearce achieved: she found the room 'finely adorned with paintings and obelisks and made as light as a summer's day'. When the Duke returned to England he took some of the decorations home with him. During his term of office a major programme of clearing and rebuilding was begun. It is principally to the works of those years that the castle owes its present tidy red-brick Georgian appearance – the shape in which it saw the giddy heyday and decline of Viceregal Ireland.

The Viceregal Levées and Drawingroom nights were the acme of social life in Ireland. To them thronged the Establishment nobility and gentry, and such merchants as could gain entrance. Those Irish who mingled with the Establishment without actually conforming, later rather perjoratively called 'Castle Catholics', also attended the social events. Customarily a ball was given each year to celebrate the Battle of the Boyne when 'The Glorious Memory of King William' was toasted. At one of these occasions a Catholic belle, the daughter of a rich Dublin brewer, came wearing a corsage of orange lilies. This provoked a witty extemporaneous eulogy from the Viceroy, Lord Chesterfield:

> Say lovely Tory, why the jest
> Of wearing orange at thy breast,
> When that same breast betraying shows
> The whiteness of the rebel rose.

Hanoverian Dublin was a gay and rowdy capital. Minor squireens, rakes, charlatans and expensive whores frequently managed to enter polite society, and the castle receptions were invariably a boisterous crush. Bibulous guests were no rarity, nor was it uncommon to see ladies in their finery scrambling on the floor to snatch sweetmeats which had fallen from the tables. By Victorian times decorum prevailed. The season began with a Levée, an evening Drawingroom, and a Banquet, on three successive days early in February, and finished on 17 March with the St Patrick's Ball, for which any person who had attended a Levée or Drawingroom was entitled to apply to the Chamberlain for an invitation. The bemedalled and bejewelled dinner guests assembled to await the formal entry of the Viceroy and Vicereine, who walked in to the strains of 'The Roast Beef of Old England'. One hundred and twenty guests frequently sat at the dinners; more would arrive for the balls which followed, at which supper would be served to eight hundred persons. Altogether, during the busy five-week season, as many as fifteen thousand people were entertained in the castle.

The castle has had a chapel since its earliest days. One is first mentioned in 1225, when Henry III approved the appointment of a chaplain. The present chapel adjoining the Record Tower was begun in 1807 to replace an earlier one that was pulled down. The Viceroy, the Duke of Bedford, laid the foundation stone on 15 February 1807, and it took seven years to complete at a cost of £42,000. The architect Francis Johnston and those associated with the decoration, like Richard Stewart who did much of the elaborate wood-carving, Edward Smyth the sculptor and Michael Stapleton the stuccodore, must surely have been delighted on Christmas Eve of 1814 when a leading Dublin newspaper, *Saunders' Newsletter*, proclaimed it to be 'the most beautiful modern specimen of the Gothic style of Architecture in Europe'.

The castle now houses Government Departments. In 1943 the chapel was adapted for Catholic services.

Dunamase Castle CO. LEIX

On the site of an Irish fort of the Early Christian era, on top of the hill of Dunamase, the Anglo-Norman invaders erected a castle first mentioned in 1215, at which time Geoffrey Lutterel was ordered by King John to cede it to William Marshall, Earl of Pembroke. It may then have been only a timber construction. In the partition of the Earl's vast estates in 1247 the Manor of Dunamase was assigned to his grand-daughter, Maud de Braose, who married Roger de Mortimer in that same year. Shortly after this, according to *Clyn's Annals,* Lysaght O'More forcibly expelled the English from his patrimony, burning eight castles in one night and destroying Roger de Mortimer's Dunamase. Subsequently de Mortimer recaptured the place and refortified it. On the summit of the hill vestiges remain of a long rectangular tower which appears to date from the thirteenth century. It stands in an inner ward, protected by a curtain wall with a gateway flanked by towers. Outside this wall was the further protection of the walled outer ward or bailey, also with a gate. Between these fortifications and the road below are a series of defensive banks and ditches which may date from the period of the earliest fort on the hill.

The castle, now very ruinous, has changed hands many times. In the Civil War it was dismantled by the Cromwellians, then partially restored as a residence. It has long been abandoned.

*The castle on the rock of Dunamase, commanding
the pass through the West Leinster hills*

Dundrum Castle CO. DOWN

When John de Courcy landed with his knights in south-east Ulster he soon conquered a considerable territory and looted the treasure of the local magnates. Between his arrival in Ireland in 1177 and his expulsion in 1204, de Courcy endowed religious establishments, built abbeys for the Benedictines and the Cistercians, and built for himself a stronghold, Dundrum Castle, then known as Rath. The Norman adventurer picked a perfect site, one that had already held a Celtic fortress, a natural mound on top of a two-hundred-foot-high hill overlooking an inlet of Dundrum Bay, the plains of Lecale and the pass between the Mountains of Mourne and the foothills of Slieve Croob.

De Courcy threw a strong polygonal curtain wall around the level summit. Whether the Norman *donjon*, the great circular keep within the ward thus created, was built or even begun by de Courcy is uncertain. It could have been the work of his immediate successors. Its plan and construction demonstrate the remarkable advances in military science and architecture achieved by the knights who had been on the Crusades. It is similar to the keep built at Pembroke in Wales about 1200 by the Earls Marshal and is the best example of its kind in Ireland. It consists of two storeys with wooden floors above a basement, with the original entrance on the first floor. Chambers and passages were constructed in the thickness of the eight-foot walls, and also a mural stair rising to the wall-walk. The internal diameter of the keep is 46 feet, and it is 52 feet high.

In the year after his expulsion, de Courcy attempted to recapture his castle with the help of his father-in-law, the King of Man, but he was unsuccessful and it became Crown property. In 1210 it was visited by King John, who sanctioned payments of small sums to a carpenter, a quarrier, a ditcher and miners for work on the castle. Later the King paid Roger Pipard, Baron of Ardee and later Seneschal of Ulster, to maintain a garrison there. For more than a century the castle was held by the Crown, or by the de Lacy and de Burgo Earls of Ulster. A gate-house was inserted in the curtain wall during the latter half of the thirteenth century, with a pair of two-storey towers flanking the entrance, over which there was a chamber. A stair outside one tower apparently led to the wall-walk along the parapets. About the same time a spacious lower ward was created by enclosing with a curtain wall a part of the hillside below the upper ward on the south-east.

For over two centuries from 1346 the history of the castle is barely documented. It appears that the Magennises seized Dundrum some time in the latter half of the fourteenth century and held it intermittently until it was surrendered to the Crown by Phelim Magennis in 1601. Raibhilin Savage was said to have been the owner when the Earl of Kildare took it in 1517; and when the Lord Deputy, Lord Leonard Grey, captured Dundrum in 1538 it was defended by a garrison of Scots placed there by Savage. Lord Grey wrote: 'I also took a castle in M'Guinous country called Doundrome, which is one of the strongest holds in Ireland and most commodious for the defence of the whole country of Lecayle both by sea and land for

Lecayle is environed by the sea and there is no way to enter it by land but by the said castle.'

After its surrender to the Crown in 1601 the castle was granted to Edward, Lord Cromwell, in 1605, then sold in 1636 by his grandson, Thomas, first Earl of Ardglass, to Sir Francis Blundell. In the Rising of 1641 the Magennises retrieved Dundrum, but it was recaptured by the Parliamentarians, who partly demolished it in 1652 to render it useless. After the war the Blundells returned and built the gabled mansion whose shell still stands at the lower edge of the lower ward. The Blundell property eventually devolved on an heiress, Baroness Sandys, who married the second Marquess of Downshire. In 1954,

View over Dundrum Bay through the breached curtain wall. See Colour Plate IV

in the lifetime of the seventh Marquess, the castle and grounds were placed in State care.

Something of Dundrum's distant Celtic past seems to cling mysteriously to the castle and its wooded hillside. Perhaps more than any other place in Ireland, it suggests, too, the world of the Norman adventurers and mercenaries – conquerors and Crusaders who fortified a castle in Ulster and talked there of the palace-castles of the Seleucid rulers they had seen in the East – the world of the overmighty barons and Plantagenet kings.

Dungory Castle CO. GALWAY

The sixteenth-century castle of Dungory, near Kinvara, stands on the site of an ancient royal seat of a seventh-century King of Connaught, Guaire Aidhneach, from whom its Irish name *Dun Guaire* is derived. The site is a good natural one for a stronghold, a narrow neck of land jutting out in an inlet of Kinvara Bay. The castle is set on the *dun*, which is like a giant stepping-stone in the shallow waters; around it are springs of fresh water which originate a few miles away in the lake of Coole Park.

King Guaire was a close kinsman of St Colman of Kilmacduagh, to whom the monarch's Easter banquet was miraculously transported when the Saint finished a seven-year retreat of fasting, prayer and penitence in the bleak hills of the Burren. St Caimin of Inishcaltra was another kinsman of the King, who was also a benefactor of St Fechin and St Madoc of Fens, the last of whom was a guest in his castle. The *Book of Lecan* praises the castle as 'the fort of lasting fame', and 'the white-sheeted fort of soft stones, habitation of poets and bishops'. Guaire was renowned for his hospitality, and this must indeed have been lavish and generous, to judge by the thanks of one parting guest, a bard who composed these lines to the King on his departure:

> We depart from thee, O stainless Guaire,
> A year, a quarter and a month
> Have we sojourned with thee, O King;
> Three times fifty poets good and smooth,
> Three times fifty students in the poetic art,
> Each with a servant and a dog,
> They were all fed in the one great house;
> Each man had his separate meal,
> Each man had his separate bed.
> We never arise at early morning
> Without contentions, without calming.
> I declare to Thee, O God,
> Who canst the promise verify,
> That should we return to our own lands
> We shall visit thee again, O Guaire, tho' now we
> depart.

It is to be hoped that the King's generosity was equal to the prospect of a return visit from three hundred guests with as many servants and dogs, when they were just leaving after a stay of sixteen months.

Even allowing for poetic exaggeration, the earlier fortress must have been much larger than the rather modest tower-house built on the site in the sixteenth century by the King's lineal descendants, the O'Heyne chieftains. This is a stout, three-storey edifice with the

principal chambers as usual on the upper floors, one measuring 21 feet 9 inches by 29 feet, the other 21 feet 9 inches by 28 feet 6 inches. It stands within an irregularly shaped, six-sided bawn, built up against the west curtain wall, which has a small rectangular towerlet for a keep at its south-west corner. The builder was probably that O'Heyne, Eoghain Muirchetach, chief of his name, who was signatory to an indenture with the Lord President of Connaught, Perrot. He lived at Dungory in 1585, and was succeeded at his death in 1588 by his son Aedh, who surrendered the castle to the Crown and had it regranted to him in 1594.

The O'Heynes must have ceded the property to the Clanrickarde Burkes shortly after this, for one Oliver Martin was holding Dungory of them by 1607; it was confirmed to him by a grant of 1615. Richard Martin, Mayor of Galway, held the castle in 1642, and at the

end of the century it belonged to Oliver Martyn, Member of Parliament for Galway. Martyn enjoyed an extraordinary privilege: although a Catholic he was specially exempted by an Act of Parliament in 1710 from the harsh restrictions against Catholics which then obtained under the Penal Laws. This was to reward him for his moderation during the war, and his kindness to distressed Protestants at that time.

As the Martins (or Martyns) made Tullira their principal seat in the barony of Kiltartan, Dungory was let to tenants. According to the historical novelist Charles F. Blake-Foster, who described the castle in his *The Irish Chieftains and Their Struggle for the Crown* (1872), Colonel Daly of Raford lived at Dungory with his family in 1787, and a garrison was stationed there in 1828.

The castle then fell into disuse, and early in the present century it was roofless and without windows

The ancient tower-house which was bought by Oliver St John Gogarty to be near the Kiltartan literati, his friends Edward Martyn and Lady Gregory

or doors. The fabric however, remained intact, due largely to the care and the antiquarian interests of Edward Martyn (*see* Tullira Castle), who placed a caretaker in charge. The walls of both the castle and the bawn have survived complete. The castle was acquired by Oliver St John Gogarty, a friend of Martyn and of his neighbour Lady Gregory; he in turn sold it to Christabel, Lady Ampthill, who repaired and fitted it up as her residence with modern conveniences. It was subsequently taken over by the present owners, the Shannon Free Airport Development Company, who maintain it, keep it open to the public and put it to use for poetry-readings, recitals and medieval-style banquets.

Dunluce Castle CO. ANTRIM

Excavations have shown that the precipitous basalt rock on which Dunluce Castle stands was inhabited at least as early as the ninth century. It is not known who built the towers and walls of the castle, which appears to date from the latter half of the thirteenth century when the Anglo-Normans controlled this north coast of Antrim. The south-east and north-east towers survive, and also the south wall, perched high over the chasm which separates the rock from land. Below the castle, close to sea-level, the whole rock is penetrated by a cave and has been slowly crumbling away for centuries.

In 1513 the members of the MacQuillan clan, a ruling North Antrim family, lords of the area called 'the Route', were concentrated at Dunluce, having chosen it as their chief residence after their other stronghold, Rathmore, was burned. It appears that the MacQuillans made no additions to the castle during their occupancy. About 1555–60 they were ousted by that redoubtable Scot, Sorley Boy McDonnell, whose brother had married a daughter of the MacQuillan chief. Sorley Boy was twice evicted, first in 1565 by Shane O'Neill and again in 1584 by the Lord Deputy, Sir John Perrott. Each time Sorley Boy repossessed himself of his castle, on the second occasion slaying the English constable, Peter Carie, and most of the garrison. Perrott had plundered Sorley Boy's treasure, taking away, among other objects, the Cross of St Columcille, which he sent to Burghley suggesting that it be bestowed on Lady Walsingham or Lady Sydney to wear 'as a jewell of weight and bigness' on some gala occasion. In 1586 Sorley Boy submitted officially to the Queen and was appointed Constable of Dunluce Castle; but nevertheless he succoured and harboured some of the survivors of the Armada galleass, the *Gerona*, which foundered on the rocks between Dunluce and the Giant's Causeway with the loss of many Spanish lives. Sorley Boy salvaged cannon from the wreck which he mounted at Dunluce. He also embellished his castle with an ambitious and surprising avant-garde loggia, built parallel to the south wall. The sandstone columns of a five-bay arcade which have been excavated suggest a construction unique in Ireland but similar to one in the Italian Renaissance manner built in the 1580s by the Earl of Bothwell at Crichton Castle in Scotland. Perhaps the one at Dunluce was never finished or soon damaged, for an early seventeenth-century building was planned without regard to it.

Sorley Boy died in 1589, and in 1597 Sir John Chichester reported that Sorley Boy's sons James and Randal were 'forteffeing themselves only in Dunluce, where they have planted three peeces of ordance, demi-cannon and culvering which were had out of one of the Spanish ships . . .' The gate-house with its corbelled corner turrets in the Scottish manner dates from about this time. Despite Sir James MacSorley's questionable loyalty and Randal's marriage to the daughter of the rebel Hugh O'Neill of Tyrone, the MacDonnells obtained a grant of the Route in 1603. Sir Randal MacSorley was advanced to the peerage as Viscount Dunluce in 1618 and created Earl of Antrim in 1620. In his time a large house whose shell survives was erected in the main courtyard. This was in the style of an English manor with mullioned windows, tall gables and chimneys, and projecting bays. Here Randal the second Earl brought his English bride. She was the widow of the murdered Duke of Buckingham, the former favourite of James I and advisor to Charles I, and was accustomed to Court life in London. It is said that she never liked the wild castle of Dunluce where the incessant beating of the waves unnerved her. Her aversion to the place was further provoked by a spot of trouble in 1639 when part of the old castle collapsed during a reception and crashed into the sea, carrying with it most of the servants. According to one tradition the only survivor in the domestic quarters was a tinker who had been sitting in a window-embrasure mending pots. After the Royalist second Earl was arrested at Dunluce in 1642 the family moved out, eventually establishing their principal residence at Glenarm. However Dunluce Castle, which fell into decay, remained the property of the Earls of Antrim until 1928, when Randal the seventh Earl transferred it to the Northern Ireland Government for preservation as a National Monument.

The excavations carried out since the castle passed into State care have revealed more of the early building and uncovered the ancient floor levels.

The sandstone columns of an Italianate loggia which was an unusual part of the sixteenth-century castle. See Colour Plate VI

Dunsany Castle CO. MEATH

The castle of the nineteenth Baron Dunsany has been the seat of his ancestors in the male line since the time of the first Baron in the fifteenth century. The first Baron had inherited it through his mother Joan Cusack, heiress of the family who held the site since the Anglo-Norman invasion in the twelfth century.

Though the substantial ruin of a fortified fifteenth-century church stands in the park, the medieval castle, which guarded an approach to Dublin from the borders of the Pale, has all but disappeared in the building additions of the last three centuries. However in a ground-plan of the present castle the ancient walls can be clearly discerned, and the old flanking towers are still visible. Much of the elegant interior dates from the latter half of the eighteenth century.

The Lords Dunsany have preserved among their treasured possessions in the castle a portrait and relics of their kinsman Saint Oliver Plunkett, who was canonized in 1975.

The medieval flanking-towers remain visible, but much of the old castle is cloaked in new buildings

Dunsoghly Castle CO. DUBLIN

Sir Rowland Plunkett, Chief Justice of the King's Bench in Ireland, obtained the Manor of Dunsoghly about 1426, and either he or his son, Sir Thomas Plunkett, Chief Justice of the Court of Common Pleas, built the present castle, which stands 80 feet high, with four storeys and projecting square towers at the angles. Each floor of the main block contains a single large chamber, while three of the flanking towers contain small chambers and the fourth contains the stair. The medieval timber roof is the last one in Ireland to survive intact. It has been very useful as a model for restorations at Bunratty Castle and at the Rothe House, Kilkenny. The joints are morticed and secured by oak pins, while the secondary rafters are laid flat, rather than edgewise as in modern roofs. Sir John Plunkett, Chief Justice of the Queen's Bench, erected the little chapel adjacent to the castle in 1573. The heirs male in direct line of Sir Thomas lived at Dunsoghly Castle until the death in 1751 without male issue of Nicholas Plunkett. The descendants of his daughters, however, continued in residence until the latter part of the last century, disdainfully disregarding the inconvenience and discomfort of a real medieval castle in a changed world where imitation ancient castles were the rage.

The great tower and adjacent small chapel are both excellently preserved

Enniskillen Castle CO. FERMANAGH

The sixteenth-century poet Tadhg Dall O'Huiginn was enthusiastic in his expressions of admiration for Enniskillen and its castle, the stronghold of the Maguires: 'Alas', he wrote, 'for him that looks on Enniskillen of lightsome bays and of sweet sounding falls: for to us it is a peril, for sure it is impossible to quit it that e'er we have gazed on the white fortress with its sod of smooth greensward.' He has also left us a vivid description of life in the castle in his time. Gentlemen dispensed largesse in the courtyard; minstrels and poets crowded the hall; ladies and women-servants embroidered rare tissues or wove golden webs; fighting men were everywhere, mingling with hostages and a regiment of wrights and artificers, some finishing silver beakers, others forging weapons, staining cloaks or rugs crimson, tempering swords, rivetting spearshafts, practising bloodletting; guests listened to music or to romances recited by storytellers, or compared genealogies. At supper protocol was observed in the seating arrangements: the poet Tadhg Dall was given the seat of honour to the right of the Maguire, who was in the central place. At bedtime, couches or rushes were strewed on the floor for the gentlemen, who were also provided with down coverlets to keep out the cold.

Today the most distinctive feature of Enniskillen Castle is not the remains of the Maguires' medieval keep, which is now a three-storey, five-bay rectangular building with Georgian windows, but the attractive water-gate with its paired corbelled pepper-pot bartizans. This must date from the building activities of Captain (later Sir) William Cole, Constable of the Castle, who obtained possession of it in 1607.

Cole was a prominent undertaker in the Plantation of Ulster; in 1611 he was assigned one thousand acres in Co. Fermanagh, eighty acres of which were in the town of Enniskillen, where he became the first Provost. When Cole came to Enniskillen Castle he undoubtedly found it in a fairly ruinous state, since it had been severely battered in the struggle between the Maguires and the Crown. Captain John Dowdall had successfully besieged the stronghold in 1594, attacking, according to a contemporary account, 'by

boats, by engines, by sap, by scaling'. He had contrived an onslaught on the garrison by sending one hundred men by boat, hidden under hurdles; they managed to reach the wall of the barbican without being detected. One hundred and fifty men, women and children were slain in the attack, and the garrison surrendered. Although Dowdall repaired the breaches made by his soldiers, the castle was again under siege the next year when the Maguire recaptured it before being once again defeated and ejected.

In 1611 it was reported that Captain Cole had built a 'fair strong wall' with a wall-walk, flankers and a parapet, and had begun work on a 'fair house' on the foundations of the old keep and storehouses. Meanwhile he and his family were living in a timber house which he put up beside the fort. The old keep had had four storeys, but in the rebuilding these were reduced to three and it was roofed.

Captain Cole's water-gate has definite stylistic affinities with contemporary buildings of other Scots settlers round Lough Erne. The paired turrets with conical roofs closely resemble those of the old castle of Crom, begun in 1611 by Michael Balfour, Laird of Mountwhany in Fifeshire (and clearly depicted in an eighteenth-century drawing made before the castle was burnt in 1764). The carving of the corbelling on the water-gate is similar to that of Castle Balfour at Lisnaskea, built in 1618 by another settler from Fifeshire, Sir James Balfour. It is likely that all three buildings were the work of the same masons, and that they, too, had come from Scotland, where such work was then fashionable.

The old keep was again repaired and partially rebuilt at the end of the eighteenth century, when the castle was used as a barracks, and the present windows were inserted at that time. It is now used as a museum of local antiquities and relics of the famous Enniskillen regiments.

The water-gate with its distinctive Scottish turrets protecting the entrance from Lough Erne

Glenarm Castle CO. ANTRIM

A MacDonnell has held the lands of Glenarm for over five hundred years. The Glens of Antrim came into the possession of the MacDonnells through the marriage of John MacDonnell, who was murdered in 1427, to Margery Byset, daughter and heiress of the Lord of the Glyns. The original stronghold built in the thirteenth century stood on the bank of the Glenarm River; it was the medieval castle which Sir John Chichester reported that James and Randal MacDonnell had broken down in 1597. In 1603 Randal received a Crown grant of his hereditary lands with the obligation to build a residence in each of his four baronies. Randal's seat was then at Dunluce, and it appears that the 'castle' he built at Glenarm was an unpretentious building. A plaque commemorating its construction is now set on the nineteenth-century gate-house. It reads: 'With the leave of God this castle was built by Sir Randal McDonnell, Knight, Erle of Antrim, having to wife Dame Aellis O'Neill, in the year of our Lord God 1636. Deus est adjutor meus.'

Originally seventeenth century, the castle has features of the Gothic, Tudor and Jacobean Revivals. The romantic gatehouse, left, dated 1825, is a charming conceit, complete with portcullis, slits, and boiling-oil holes

Additions may have been made to Glenarm later in the century after the Earls of Antrim abandoned Dunluce. In 1756, the year after his third marriage, the third Earl rebuilt the castle in the Irish Palladian manner, with flanking pavilions linked to the main block by curving colonnades. None of the wives produced a son, and the property passed to the third Earl's elder daughter, Anne Catherine, Countess of Antrim. Following her second marriage in 1817, she and her new husband, a man of humble origin but decided taste, again rebuilt the castle, employing William Vitruvius Morrison as their architect. The style is generically 'Revival', including Gothick, Tudor and Jacobean features as well as Dutch gables. A fire in 1929 necessitated further rebuilding and some of the Gothick windows were removed.

Glenstal Castle CO. LIMERICK

Glenstal was designed in 1837 by William Bardwell for Sir Joseph Barrington, the founder of the Limerick Hospital and Infirmary who had been made a baronet in 1831. The cylindrical keep was finished in 1839, in Sir Joseph's lifetime, as were parts of the main house, but work dragged on on the mammoth pile for more than forty years. This was due to interruptions forced by the distress of the Famine in the 1840s and the consequent diminished income from the estates, and also by the successive deaths of Sir Joseph, his son and his grandson, in 1846, 1861 and 1872 respectively. The castle was finally completed under Sir Croker Barrington, the fourth Baronet.

The approach to the castle is through a carriage entrance inspired by the keep of a medieval castle in England. Statues of King Edward I and his Queen, Eleanor of Castile, adorn each side of the front door;

The garden front of the castle with the impressive cylindrical keep of 1839, and right, *one of the fine gargoyles, uncommon in Ireland*

the Queen holds a partly-furled scroll inscribed with the Irish words of welcome *Cead mile failte*. The numerous Celtic Revival elements at Glenstal are credited to the enthusiasm of the second Baronet, Crown Solicitor for Munster, and his wife, *née* Hartigan. They were close friends of the third Earl of Dunraven, a zealous and informed antiquarian and archaeologist who was proud of his Celtic scholarship. The ornate doorway between two of the reception rooms is a replica of the elaborate Romanesque doorway in Killaloe Cathedral; it was executed in 1841, and is one of the first pieces of Celtic Revival sculpture in the country. The doorways of the main

bedrooms are also modelled on Hiberno-Romanesque church-doorways.

Throughout the house sculpted motifs abound, borrowed from the famous sites such as Clonmacnois as depicted in the antiquarian Petrie's *Pilgrims at Clonmacnois*, or taken from O'Neill's *Illustrations of the Most Interesting Sculptured Crosses of Ancient Ireland*, published in 1857. The successive Baronets remained faithful to the Celtic theme. The staircase, gallery and balusters in dark oak are intricately carved with a profusion of Celtic interlacing, foliage and animals. This was the work of men trained at Ahane, and was executed in 1888.

Now renamed Glenstal Abbey, the castle today houses a renowned boarding school for boys kept by a community of the monks of the Order of St Benedict, which acquired the premises in 1927.

Above, *Queen Eleanor flanking the entrance-door;* left, *the curious window of the gate-lodge;* and right, *the door between two reception-rooms, copied from one in Killaloe Cathedral*

Glenveagh Castle CO. DONEGAL

The attractions of Glenveagh are its magnificent
setting and gardens, and the ambience created there
by its successive owners. In 1870 John Adair
purchased from the Earl of Leitrim twenty-two
thousand acres of rugged land in County Donegal, and
this became the vast demesne of Glenveagh Castle
which he built on the edge of Lough Veagh, encircled
by the Derryveagh and Glendowan mountains.
Hundreds of red deer now wander the slopes of

*The castle set against the gleaming hillside, from the kitchen-
garden. See Colour Plate V*

Altachoastia, Kinnaveagh and Dooish, descendants of
the herd started by Mr Adair. He and his American
wife were well-liked by the many guests, including
royalty, whom they entertained in high Victorian
state at the castle, but unfortunately Adair was less
generous as a landlord in a period of severe agricul-

120

tural distress. His acrimonious relations with his tenants led to the murder of the agent of the estate, and to many of his tenants being cruelly evicted from their homes.

The castle is constructed of rough-hewn granite. It appears to have been built in the first instance as a four-storey rectangular keep with battlemented parapets and five-foot thick walls, in medieval tradition. Two-storey wings extend from two of its sides, and attached to one wing is a circular tower. Another wing with domestic offices is joined to the south side of the house.

Despite, or perhaps because of, its remoteness, Glenveagh has attracted discerning purchasers. Professor Arthur Kingsley Porter of Harvard University, a distinguished art-historian, bought the castle in 1929, and for the few years that he lived there until his mysterious disappearance on Inishboffin one summer day, he and Mrs Porter entertained writers, artists and historians at the castle. A wealthy and brilliant young American, Mr Henry McIlhenny, whose grandfather had emigrated to the New World

from Milford, Co. Donegal, only a few miles from Glenveagh Castle, was a guest there in 1936, and after renting the castle from Mrs Porter the next summer, he bought it from her in 1938. He has expressed his love for Glenveagh in the discrimination with which he has decorated and furnished the castle, and improved the gardens with the help of well-known landscape architects such as Jim Russell and Lanning Roper. Phillipe Jullian, the French writer, arbiter of fashion and lexicographer of snobbism, designed the Gothick conservatory. The tradition of entertainment has reached its apogee under Mr McIlhenny, whose guests number international celebrities, art-collectors, artists, architects, duchesses, debutantes and dilettantes, writers, composers, tycoons, aesthetes and acolytes. Few are not enchanted by the blaze of rhododendron in June, by the statue-garden, the rose-garden, the mysterious moss-garden on the mountainside and the shimmering lake, and by the atmosphere of the house and the beauty of the furnishings.

An angle of the swimming-pool at the edge of the lough

Glin Castle CO. LIMERICK

Top, *the neat castellations and toy turrets are exclusively decorative. Above, the charming Gothick pepper-pot gate-lodge*

The medieval castle of the Knights of Glin, a cadet branch of the Fitzgeralds, Earls of Desmond, was largely destroyed by the army of the Lord President of Munster in 1600. Carew first blockaded the castle from the river, then directed his cannon at it and breached the wall. The garrison fought on with exceptional gallantry, contesting the staircase step by step with desperate resistance until they were killed on the roof or fell to death from the battlements. The rather shapeless ruin of a tower in Glin village hardly conveys the former importance of the castle. The strong keep was at one angle of a rectangular bawn with turrets at the other corners and a detached banqueting-hall. The family made some repairs in 1615, according to the inscription on a stone now set in the archway to the stables of the present castle which reads: 'Edmond Gerrald Knight of the Vally. Onnor Cartie his wife. Fear God alway and remember the Poor. I.H.S. Anno Domini 1615.'

The present castle, standing in a pleasant demesne on the outskirts of Glin overlooking the Shannon, was built by the twenty-fourth Knight and his English wife shortly after their marriage in 1789. About 1815 their son, the twenty-fifth Knight, an admirer of Gothick and Picturesque, began a process of gothicazation, adding battlements to the house and the west wing. He also built the enchanting castellated pepper-pot gate-lodges. The castle which is splendidly furnished is now the residence of the twenty-ninth Knight, a well-known Irish art-historian and writer on architecture, whose Canadian step-father Mr Milner munificently restored the place.

Glinsk Castle CO. GALWAY

This handsome four-storey strong-house of the Burkes of Glinsk appears to have been built about the middle of the seventeenth century, possibly during the years of the Catholic Confederacy in the 1640s. It is a double-pile of three bays, with finely sculpted mullioned windows and tall, elegant chimneys. The plan is a rectangle with two square towers projecting from the south front. Although these towers have corner machicolations the defences of the castle are surprisingly frail. Nevertheless, the house has a distinctly fortified air, differing greatly from contemporary country houses in England where, apart from the Civil War, the proprietors did not expect to have to resist sporadic attacks and skirmishes.

A fine example of the seventeenth-century fortified mansion

Gosford Castle CO. ARMAGH

Gosford, near Markethill, is the first Norman Revival castle to be built in the British Isles. Begun in 1819, it thus predates Hopper's better known neo-Norman castle at Penrhyn in Wales by about ten years. The second Earl of Gosford, who served as Governor of Canada, employed as architect Thomas Hopper, also patronized by the Prince Regent, later George IV, for whom he designed the ornate Gothick conservatory at Carlton House, London. When it was completed after twenty years, Gosford was claimed to be the largest country house in Ireland – a massive complex of circular towers, angular keep, bastions, towerlets and arches linked internally by rambling corridors. Pale granite quarried at Bessbrook in Co. Armagh was used for its construction. The Norman theme is pursued purposefully and executed with masterful originality.

After the sale of its contents in 1921 the castle was used by the army. Soldiers were billeted there, and during the Second World War it served as a place of internment for German prisoners-of-war. It is now being repaired and restored by the Government.

Its former owners the Acheson family, later Earls of Gosford, received large grants of land in Co. Armagh in 1611 during the Plantation of Ulster, and the castle stands in a magnificent demesne of 580 acres. Dean Swift as a guest of the Achesons planned garden-walks and other improvements. The estate is now a Forest Park and open to the public, who can enjoy the arboretum, the nature trail and the camping and picnic facilities.

Right, the entrance, and below, the garden-front of the largest castle-country house in Ireland, which has an endless maze of corridors and stairs

Granagh Castle CO. KILKENNY

The three round turrets and linking curtain wall rising above the River Suir are part of the original castle built by the Le Poers in the thirteenth century, when cylindrical towers and keeps were in fashion. Turrets and wall formed one side of the external fortifications which surrounded a square enclosure.

The other ruinous buildings, a tall square keep of the fourteenth or fifteenth century, in which an attractive oriel window was inserted in the seventeenth century, and a detached two-storey hall with vestiges of fine sculptural ornamentation, were built by the Butlers of Ormond. The figure of St Michael the Archangel in one of the chambers suggests that it was used as a chapel. Edmund Le Poer granted Granagh to Sir James Le Botiller, Earl of Ormond, about 1330, and its possession by the Earls of Ormond was confirmed by a grant of the Manor of Granagh by Letters Patent of King Edward III in 1375.

Cromwell's troops who took the castle in the Civil War partly demolished it. Subsequently the local peasantry quarried the site for building materials. Its present state of preservation is due to the zeal of George Roch who, stimulated by the prevailing renewal of interest in medieval buildings, paid a Waterford mason to make necessary repairs in 1827.

The curtain wall and thirteenth-century turret

Green Castle CO. DOWN

As it was originally built half-way through the thirteenth century, the keep of *Viride Castrum*, standing on a hillock overlooking Carlingford Lough, was in a style already fifty years or more out of date in England. Completed about 1261, when payments were made by the Crown for timber, shingles and lead for the roof, the keep was rectangular, and had two storeys with the entrance on the first floor. Only fragments of the curtain wall survive. Like Carlingford Castle across the lough, Green Castle belonged to the King, and was entrusted to the care of the de Burghs, Earls of Ulster.

Important alliances were arranged for the daughters of Richard de Burgh, the Red Earl. One, Elizabeth, was Queen of Scotland, the wife of Robert Bruce; another married the Earl of Desmond, while the marriages of a third daughter, Joan, and a fourth, Catherine, to the second Earl of Kildare and Sir Maurice de Burgh respectively were celebrated in Green Castle on successive days in the summer of 1312. Only four years later the castle was sacked by Edward Bruce as

he rampaged through Ulster. It was subsequently recovered for the King, but the rule of the de Burghs ended with the murder of William, the last Earl of Ulster of that dynasty.

Throughout the fourteenth century, after Earl William's death, Green Castle was repeatedly attacked and damaged by the Irish, who on more than one occasion managed to eject the constable and garrison.

In 1505 the Lord Deputy, Gerald, eighth Earl of Kildare, was granted Green Castle as part of his reward for having defeated a confederacy of rebellious Irish chiefs at the Battle of Knock Tuagh. It may have been in his time or shortly before that the castle was enlarged and strengthened. The walls of the keep were raised to make another storey with square angle-turrets rising above it, and an entrance was made on the west front to replace the one on the first floor.

The House of Kildare fell from favour after the rebellion of the Silken Thomas, and in 1542 Sorley Boy McDonnell petitioned to have Green Castle given to him. The authorities deemed it wiser to wait and give it to a subject of more proven loyalty. It was granted together with Carlingford to Sir Nicholas Bagnall in 1552, when he replaced the narrow lights with the large windows in the great hall on the first floor, and inserted the fireplace. The Bagnall family continued to live there for several generations, and added the domestic quarters once clustered about the keep. The castle is now in State care.

The keep, a fine example of Norman military architecture

VIII Killymoon Castle CO. TYRONE

Killymoon was one of the castles designed by the English architect John Nash before he transformed parts of London such as Regent's Park and Regent Street. *See* p. 156.

IX Johnstown Castle CO. WEXFORD

A nineteenth-century Revival castle beside a romantic artificial lake. It incorporates medieval and seventeenth-century buildings. *See* p. 142.

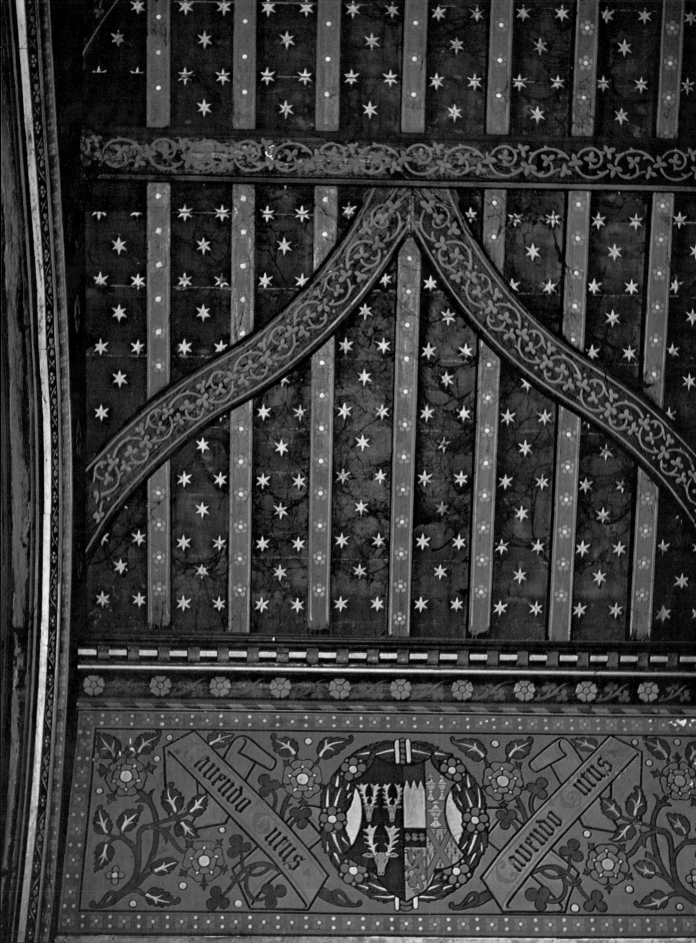

X Kylemore Castle CO. GALWAY

The baronial castle built by a nineteenth-century
tycoon, once famed for its hospitality in the Edwar-
dian grand manner. It is now an abbey of Benedictine
nuns. *See* p. 160.

XI Lismore Castle CO. WATERFORD

The ducal seat was embellished in the nineteenth
century by the great architect Pugin, who decorated
the banqueting-hall like a chapel. *See* p. 168.

Grianan of Ailech

CO. DONEGAL

This magnificent stone fort dates from the early centuries of Christianity in Ireland, although legend would have it that it was built by the gods of antiquity. Possibly the site was a druidic holy place before the northern O'Neills chose it as their royal seat. Their kings reigned there from about the fifth century, and it must have been from this spot that Flaithbhertach O'Neill, King of Ailech, surnamed 'of the Pilgrim's staff', set out for his pilgrimage to Rome in 1029/30. The fort was wrecked in 1101 when Muirchertach O'Brien, King of Munster, marched north with his army and attacked the O'Neills to avenge the destruction of his own seat, Kincora near Killaloe in Co. Clare. It is related that to make his victory complete he gave orders that each of his men should carry off from the fort one of its stones.

The fort represents the culmination of a building tradition emerging from the hill-forts of the Iron Age. A stone wall encloses a spacious hill-top area which is further protected by an encompassing ditch. Sometimes such forts were constructed over a necropolis of the Bronze Age.

Grianan of Ailech and the stone fort at Staigue in Co. Kerry are among the most imposing examples in Ireland. Even so, they are less magnificent than Dun Aengus on Inishmore in the Aran Islands (p. 10) which is the most impressive primitive fortification in Western Europe.

The Grianan is encircled by three low concentric walls which are part of the original fortification. The enclosure is 77 feet in diameter, and the tall, massive walls contain chambers within their thirteen-foot thickness. Access to the fort is through a long, lintelled tunnel. Steps on the interior walls lead to wall-walks on the ramparts which command an extensive view over Lough Foyle and Lough Swilly.

Unfortunately the site was a victim of the wave of archaeological interest in the last century, when it was reconstructed by an enthusiastic doctor from Derry who did not keep drawings of how it had appeared before he embarked on his alterations.

The ramparts of the ancient hill-fort commanding a vast sweep of surrounding countryside. Inside, the walls, reconstructed by an amateur archaeologist in the last century, recall an amphitheatre of classical antiquity

Gurteen-le-Poer CO. WATERFORD

John William Power of Gurteen, the scion of a family established in the county since the Anglo-Norman invasion, began work on a new mansion on his lands after the death of his father in 1830. His first intention seems to have been a neoclassical house, as witness the delightful little gate-lodges in that style on the front and back avenues. Progress was slow. By 1837 only the stables had been completed. The Famine interrupted the work, and then when Mr Power died in 1851, building was left in abeyance until his son Edmond James came of age in 1862. This young gentleman, Chamberlain to Pope Pius IX who created him a Count in 1864, was steeped in medieval nostalgia. Harking back to the far-off Norman

The architect included a tower, turrets, fancy parapets and mullioned bays to suit the taste of a nineteenth-century papal chamberlain

antecedents of his family he changed his surname to de la Poer by Royal Licence in 1863. His castle, completed in 1866, reveals this nostalgia, but the medley of Revival styles lacks serious historicism. Generically Tudor Revival with gables, it has a fanciful mock-Norman keep; the great hall and gallery have lofty Gothic arches. The present owner is Edmond, the third Count, the grandson of Edmond, the first Count.

Hillsborough Fort CO. DOWN

The delightful twin-towered Gothick castle, two storeys in height with battlemented parapets, was built as a garden-house about 1758. The flanking turrets are strongly battered at their base and contain small rooms. The three-bay central block has a single spacious hall on the upper floor and living-rooms disposed around an entrance hall on the ground floor.

The topographer Samuel Lewis, writing in 1837, thought this building to have been the one where King William III slept when his army was encamped near Hillsborough, and where he issued the declaration granting the Regium Donum to the Presbyterian ministers in Ulster. In fact, the eighteenth-century castle was built on the base of a square seventeenth-century tower, and the earlier building would have been the one associated with King William.

The tower was at the entrance to an artillery fort built in the 1650s by the enterprising Colonel Arthur Hill, ancestor of the Marquesses of Downshire. Colonel of a regiment under Charles I, he served in Parliament under Cromwell, survived the Restoration purges and was a Privy Councillor under Charles II. The fort became a Royal garrison in 1660, and in that year Colonel Hill was appointed hereditary constable with twenty warders. His heirs kept up their hereditary office and maintained the fort, which was kept garrisoned and also used as an armoury for the Down yeomanry.

The plan of the fort is a star-shape, with four strong spear-shaped bastions projecting from the angles of a 270 foot square enclosure to command the old Dublin-Belfast-Carrickfergus road. The present castle stands in the middle of one of the stone-faced mud ramparts which formed part of the defence of the fort. A wall-walk ran along the top of these ramparts, behind a parapet.

A Gothick castellated garden-house in avant-garde eighteenth-century fashion

Howth Castle CO. DUBLIN

The St Lawrences of Howth, like the Talbots of Malahide, are found still in possession in the twentieth century of the lands their ancestor obtained soon after the Anglo-Norman invasion of Ireland in the twelfth century. So ancient is the lordship of Howth that there is confusion and uncertainty in the enumeration of the thirty or thirty-one St Lawrence Lords of Howth, down to the last male of the direct line, who died in 1909. The present owner of Howth Castle, Mr Gaisford-St Lawrence, descends from the last lord's elder sister, Lady Emily Gaisford. Technically the barony was a peerage by prescription, that is to say, it was one of those ancient baronies recognized in 1489 by Henry VII. Christopher St Lawrence, Baron of Howth, who did homage for his lands in 1437, was granted a licence in 1451 to search for a mine within his lordship; later he was appointed Constable of Dublin Castle for life. The lands and title were confirmed to Nicholas St Lawrence, Lord Chancellor of Ireland, in 1489; he died in 1526 and was succeeded by his son Christopher who then moved his residence from Baldongan Castle to Howth Castle, where he died in 1542.

For forty years in the reign of Elizabeth I another Christopher, 'the Blind Lord', was Lord of Howth; he built additions to the ancient keep. This Christopher was a violent and evil-tempered man; in 1579 he was convicted, fined and imprisoned for beating his wife with extreme cruelty because she had reprimanded him for his dissolute life, and upbraided him for his neglect of her although she had borne him fourteen children. There is a story that Grace O'Malley, 'the Pirate Queen', put into Howth harbour and came to the castle for hospitality in the time of this Chris-topher. He was at table and ordered that she be sent away. She, wild with fury at this rebuff, kidnapped the heir, Nicholas St Lawrence, and sailed off to her dominions in the western isles of Mayo. Eventually the boy was restored to his family on condition that the castle gates should never again be shut at mealtimes, and that a place should always be set at table for the chief of the O'Malleys. The custom, a known medieval one of laying a place for a possible uninvited guest, is still observed.

During the Civil War the St Lawrences contrived to avoid ejection by the Cromwellians. The Baron, while professing his readiness to serve the King, refused to take part in the Catholic Confederacy. Later in the century the Lord behaved with similar dexterity; he sat in the Irish Parliaments of James II and then signed the declaration in favour of William III. His son, who succeeded in 1727, a friend of Dean Swift, rebuilt Howth Castle in 1738, adding to the front the pedimented doorway, the terrace and the steps.

The fosse which once surrounded the castle was filled in during the last century.

The western tower was designed by Sir Edwin Lutyens, who also built a chapel at the end of the south-east range of the castle and made alterations to three small panelled rooms to create the present dining-room, and laid out the herbaceous garden on the south side.

A tower of the medieval castle. Howth has been the residence of one family for eight hundred years

Humewood Castle CO. WICKLOW

One of the most remarkable Victorian buildings in Ireland, Humewood was designed by the eccentric and controversial architect William White. It brought him fame, but not so much for his design as for the lawsuit brought against him by the contractor when the cost far exceeded the estimate and the owner refused to pay.

The commission came from the Right Honourable William Wentworth Fitzwilliam Dick of Humewood, Member of Parliament for Co. Wicklow and a former High Sheriff of the county, who had assumed his mother's family surname of Dick in lieu of his own, Hume, in 1864.

It appears that Mr Dick had in mind a much more modest building when he invited White to Wicklow in 1866 to examine the site. It is incredible, seeing Humewood Castle as it was built, to discover that he wanted 'an occasional resort in the summer recess or shooting season' when he visited his estate in Ireland. An English building-contractor, Albert Kimberley, tendered an estimate of £13,650 based on White's first sketches.

A masterly composition of rectangular and triangular forms, with the usual Victorian attention to the skyline. Below, the view across the stable yard; and right, *from the top of the tower. See Colour Plate VII*

White continued to enlarge and improve his original designs, and Mr Dick, ingenuously believing that all would be covered by the original estimate, watched his castle grow without interference. When in 1870 he received the builder's bill for £25,000 and refused to pay the difference, Kimberley sued White and Dick and won.

The castle is built of granite, a material which White knew and liked. 'In the treatment of granite especial care is required to make the mouldings of a broad, bold and massive, rather than a small or delicately undercut character, and to avoid as far as possible anything like minuteness and pettiness in the finish,' wrote White, and he has observed his own dictum at Humewood. It is a masterful composition of triangular and pyramidal forms, building up to the turret rising above the corner of the rectangular central tower. The stable block received the same skilful treatment.

An impressive skyline is a characteristic of Victorian architecture and White subscribed to its importance. 'For exterior effect our attention must be directed to the sky outline before expending it upon minutiae,' he commented, adding that this was particularly important when the site was in undulating country. At Humewood he achieved a restless silhouette of horizontals and curves, crenellated towers, spirelets and gables dramatically set against the backdrop of the Wicklow mountains.

Like Godwin, who was engaged on Dromore at the same time, White paid attention to the danger of attack by the Fenians. This was a justification for the basement with strongly-barred windows, which also served to keep the damp from the main part of the house. Another useful feature for defence was the porte-cochère. Guards in the room above it could command the entrance through firing holes pierced in the vaulted roof of the porch.

Mr Dick, who had apparently abandoned all idea of 'an occasional resort', employed another architect, James Brooks, to make additions and changes. The nursery wing at the north end was raised and transformed into a vast banqueting-hall, two storeys high. A tower to provide additional rooms for menservants was added to the stable-block. The most imposing room of all White's imposing Victorian interior, rich in unique details and redolent of splendour and immutable security, is the entrance-hall with its heraldic stained glass and colossal black Kilkenny marble columns.

The present owner is Mrs Hume-Weygand, whose father William Hume Hume succeeded to the property by devise on the death of Mr Dick in 1892.

Johnstown Castle CO. WEXFORD

Nineteenth-century Gothic Revival Johnstown Castle was built on to an earlier castle which included a three-storey medieval tower-house of the Esmonde family. The Esmondes had owned the estate before the Cromwellian confiscations, when a Lieutenant-Colonel Overstreet was granted the place in lieu of arrears of pay. Overstreet's widow and her second husband settled the estate on John Reynolds, a Wexford merchant. Either he or his daughter Mary, who married John Grogan in 1682, built a three-storey five-bay castellated mansion in the seventeenth century. The old Esmonde tower-house became one of the projecting flanking towers of this house, and a matching flanker was built on the opposite side.

In the second decade of the nineteenth century John Knox Grogan had a new block, three storeys above a basement, built and joined to the south and east sides of the existing castle, thus giving it a new south front with great flanking cylindrical towers. Subsequently a laboratory was erected, linked to the east side of the castle by a Tudor-style arcade. Two tall octagonal towers were also added at that period, one to the west of the laboratory, the other on the north

Above, the fortified port-cochère and graceful octagonal turrets; right, exuberant Revival detail in the passage from the main block to the ballroom. See Colour Plate IX

side of the main building. During the Famine years Hamilton K. Grogan-Morgan provided much-needed work by building the porte-cochère surmounted by a square tower. Then the laboratory wing was extended northwards to accommodate a ballroom with a billiard room and chapel above it. Later a small two-storey nursery wing was added to the south-west of the castle and integrated with the rest of the buildings by another octagonal tower built on to its west wall.

The castle and lands were sold by auction in 1944 after the death of Lady Maurice Fitzgerald, the granddaughter of Hamilton K. Grogan-Morgan. They were purchased for an Agricultural Institute by the Ministry of Agriculture, who undertook to preserve unaltered the magnificently wooded ornamental park of fifty acres, which include three artificial lakes. These grounds are now open to the public, and, with the castle, are protected by an Act of Parliament, to give pleasure for many years to come.

Kanturk Castle CO. CORK

Unfinished Kanturk was the ambitious project of a native Irish chieftain who built a fortress to vie with those of the Establishment. When the Irish chiefs were summoned to a Parliament in Dublin in 1585 two rival contenders appeared claiming the lordship of Duhallow and the chiefship of the MacDonogh branch of the MacCarthy clan. One, Donogh MacCormac Oge MacDonogh, was recognized as the rightful claimant by the Chief of the MacCarthys, Florence MacCarthy Mor; it was the other, however, Dermot MacOwen MacDonogh, who emerged within a few years as the MacDonogh, and in possession of Duhallow.

Carew, the Lord President of Munster, described this Dermot as 'a man for wit and courage nothing inferior to any of the Munster rebels' and as 'a gentleman of great land'. He was one of the signatories to a letter to the Pope denouncing the Queen's government as worse than that of the Pharaohs, yet in the summer of 1601 he professed loyalty to the Queen, asking the Lord President for her protection and promising in return his loyalty and obedience. Dermot's sincerity must always have been doubted by the authorities, for when Carew asked him what he would do if the Spaniards landed, the Chief boldly replied: 'Your Lordship puts me a hard question for if that should happen let not your Lordship trust me or the Lords Barry or Roche, or any other whatsoever that you have best conceit of, for if you do you will be deceived.' Within a month of Dermot's act of submission the Spaniards did land at Kinsale. He marched to join them with five hundred fighting men, kerne, gallowglasses and cavalry.

It is not surprising, therefore, that when this powerful chief erected an impressive castle on his lands it excited the fears and suspicions of his English neighbours, and that the Government ordered him to stop the work.

The building, a great rectangular central block, four storeys in height, flanked at each corner by communicating square five-storey towers, remains unfinished, although the masons reached the corbels which were to carry the parapets. It is not clear whether the work was left uncompleted in obedience to the mandate of the authorities, or because of Dermot MacDonogh's financial troubles which followed. The appearance of the castle illustrates a transition, slow to emerge in Ireland, from the late medieval tower-house style to that of a tudor mansion with rows of mullioned transom-windows, plentiful fireplaces and decorative refinements like the handsome carved stone doorcase set in a round-headed doorway.

Dermot was taken prisoner after the Irish defeat at Kinsale but was pardoned in 1604, and in 1615 received a grant of his hereditary territory of Duhallow, including Kanturk, by Letters Patent. Possibly in order to pay for the castle, he borrowed from Sir Philip Percival more money than the Manor of Kanturk and the other lands were worth. Percival foreclosed and entered into possession of the estates. In the 1641 Rising, Dermot, who must then have been well over seventy, threw in his lot with the rebels, thereby losing even his equity of redemption of his former property.

The castle, an empty shell with a 'built-to-last-forever' look, is now a National Monument.

The unfinished strong-house of a powerful chieftain. Below, *a handsome doorway, a rare departure from the functional and defensive in Elizabethan Ireland.* Right, *the interior of the great gaunt shell*

Kilcash Castle CO. TIPPERARY

James, ninth Earl of Ormond, granted the lands of Kilcash to his third son John Butler by deed dated 26 May 1544, and it was probably at that time that the tower-house with bartizans and tall chimneys was built on the slopes of Slievenamon. Beside it stands the ruin of a two-storey domestic building added to provide more comfortable accommodation. Kilcash Castle became the seat of this branch of the Butler family. Sir Walter Butler of Kilcash, a devout Catholic, inherited the earldom as eleventh Earl in 1614, but was prevented from enjoying the Ormond estates and spent eight years in prison. Sir Walter's elder grandson eventually regained his rights, and became twelfth Earl, first Duke of Ormonde, and Viceroy of Ireland under Charles II. Kilcash went to his younger brother, Richard Butler, who received a confirmation of it for himself and his male heirs in 1639. Richard Butler's descendants continued to live in Kilcash Castle until the death of John Butler of Kilcash in 1766, when, the senior branch of the Ormonde family having by then died out, the earldom devolved on the Kilcash branch, the lands once again became part of the vast Ormonde estate, and Kilcash Castle fell into disuse.

The seat of a cadet branch of the Butlers of Ormond

Kilcolman Castle CO. CORK

Under the scheme for the plantation of the confiscated Desmond lands in Munster with English Protestants loyal to the Crown, a perpetual lease of 3,028 acres including the lands and castle of Kilcolman near Doneraile was granted in 1586 to Edmund Spenser, the 'Prince of Poets'. A Londoner, a graduate of Cambridge and a rabid anti-papist, Spenser had demonstrated his firmness and his loyalty when, as secretary to the Lord Deputy, he had participated in the brutal massacre of the expeditionary force of six hundred Italians and Spaniards who had surrendered unconditionally at Smerwick in 1580.

Spenser held a post in the Dublin Court of Chancery which he resigned in 1588, at which time he probably took up residence at Kilcolman. He was certainly there in the summer of 1589 when he received the visit of Sir Walter Ralegh, who immediately recognized his talent and perceived the merit of the first three books of *The Faerie Queen*. Although Spenser had so little sympathy for the Irish, he was far from insensitive to the enchantment of the Munster countryside. The Awbeg River which flows near Kilcolman is the 'Mulla' of his verse, and the inspiration of Irish names, landscape and castles permeates his work.

Apart from visits to England, Spenser lived at Kilcolman until 1598. The four-storey tower-house had probably been built by the sixth Earl of Desmond when he received the property from an uncle in 1418; it appears from the ruins that there were some later additions to the original tower. Such a defensible building with scant comfort was the usual abode of a settler in the sixteenth century, for danger of attack was ever present. Kilcolman Castle was attacked and burned by insurgents at the Rising in 1598; the poet and his family fled to Cork and thence to England.

As well as his *Veue of the State of Ireland* (1596) and memoranda on the Irish situation, Spenser wrote poetry during his 'Kilcolman period': the fourth, fifth and sixth books of *The Faerie Queen,* the *Amoretti* (love-sonnets of his courtship of his second wife Elizabeth Boyle), and the *Epithalamion,* commemorating their marriage on Midsummer's Day of 1594.

Spenser's son sold his interest in Kilcolman to Sir William St Leger in 1630. It is doubtful whether the castle has been inhabited since the fire of 1598, in which some of Spenser's manuscripts may have perished, including a seventh book of *The Faerie Queen* of which only fragments are known.

Now overgrown and ruined, the Munster home of the poet Edmund Spenser

Kilkenny Castle

The *Annals of Innisfallen* record under the year 1173 an expedition by Domhnall O'Brien, King of Thomond, against the castle of Kilkenny and the 'Foreigners' (i.e. Norman invaders) who dwelt in it. According to the annalist the foreigners fled to Waterford and the Irish plundered the whole district. Kilkenny was at that time the territory of Richard, Earl of Pembroke, better known as Strongbow, the pretender to the Kingdom of Leinster through his marriage to Eva (Aoife), the daughter of King Dermot who had died at Ferns in 1171. Strongbow held court at Kildare, and it would appear that his castle at Kilkenny was then no more than a fortification of earth (motte) of the kind favoured by the Normans in Ireland during the early years of their conquest of the country. The site was high ground above the River Nore to the south-east of the settlement which already existed there, clustered around the ancient monastery of St Canice (Cainaeach) from whom the town derives its name.

Strongbow was succeeded by his son-in-law, William, the Earl Marshal, husband of his heiress-

Seen from across the River Nore, the castle as it was rebuilt in the 1820s, incorporating the medieval drum-towers and parts of the old walls

daughter Isabel. When William returned from the Crusades to Ireland in 1207 to administer his wife's vast inheritance, he chose Kilkenny as his chief seat. The first stone castle there was built during his period of residence, from 1207–13, after which his duties called him to England where he was one of the signatories of the Magna Carta, an executor of King John's will and Regent of the Realm during the minority of King Henry III. He died in England in 1219. It is to be expected that such a potentate would build an important seat, and his great fortress with a drum-shaped tower at each corner of an irregular rectangle has imposed its plan on all later building. Three of the angle-towers survive, although their form has been altered. The north wall is still that of the original building.

The vast Irish estates of the Earl Marshal were divided among his five daughters by an act of partition dated 9 May 1247. The *caput baroniae*, the castle of Kilkenny, was assigned to Isabel, the first of the five, and passed to her descendants the Despencers, who did not, however, reside in Ireland. An Inquisition of 1307 lists among the lands of Joan, Countess of Gloucester and Hereford, in the town of Kilkenny, the castle with 'una aula, quatuor turres, una capella, una mota, et alie domus diverse ad idem castrum necessarie' (a hall, four towers, a chapel, a moat and divers other houses necessary to the same castle).

During the thirteenth to fourteenth centuries Kilkenny was second only in importance to Dublin. Parliament frequently met in the castle, and in 1366 drew up the famous Statutes of Kilkenny which endeavoured to preserve the Englishness of the Pale by prohibiting marriage between colonists of English descent and the original Irish, the use by the colonists of Irish surnames, language or costume and the admission of Irish priests and religious to foundations under Anglo-Norman control.

In 1391–2 James Butler, third Earl of Ormond, who had lost his castles of Nenagh and Rosecrea further west, purchased the manor and castle of Kilkenny and other Despencer fiefs of the absentee proprietors and made his capital there. Under the Butlers, Earls of Ormond, Kilkenny flourished and grew in importance, due both to their power and to its strategic position. Undoubtedly they made embellishments to the ancient castle, for they were the most travelled and cosmopolitan of the nobles of the late medieval period, but all trace of their improvements or decoration has vanished under later changes.

In 1642–8 Kilkenny was virtually the capital of the country. The castle was the seat of Government and the headquarters of the Catholic Confederacy. The Papal Nuncio Rinuccini was splendidly received there in 1645, when the struggle to unite all the Irish in a common cause was carried on against a background of deceit, intrigue, interdictions, excommunications and conflicting loyalties. Rinuccini, having failed in his mission, returned to Rome. The nobles of Ireland failed to unite against Cromwell, the common enemy, and he, progressing in his brutal and successful campaign, besieged the castle in March 1650. After five days' siege the garrison surrendered.

At the Restoration the Marquess of Ormonde returned from his exile to serve as Viceroy and become the first Duke of Ormonde. Both he and his Duchess were enthusiastic builders and patrons. At Kilkenny he rebuilt the ancient castle, retaining the outline

dictated by the outer walls and towers, but attempting by remodelling to make it fashionable and closer in appearance to châteaux he had admired in France. He had stone brought from Caen in Normandy where he had spent time in exile; it was landed at Inistioge and brought by smaller boats up the Nore to Kilkenny. French artisans were also imported. In 1679 the steward Captain John Baxter reported that the courtyard was paved, the Duke's apartment nearly ready and that marble piers for the grotto, chimney-pieces for the castle, and 145 trees for the garden had

The north front with the incongruous balconies added to soften its grim appearance

149

arrived. Grinling Gibbons submitted a design for an iron gate in 1681, and the next year a fountain was set up. However the Duke went to England where he spent the last years of his life, so that his work at Kilkenny remained uncompleted.

His son, the second Duke, a distinguished general, resumed the work on the castle when he returned to Ireland to serve as Viceroy in 1703. He erected a handsome gate-house in the classical style, of which the pedimented and pilastered façade survives as the present entrance to the courtyard. The whole gate-house appears in a view drawn about 1816 for the architect William Robertson. Dr Thomas Molyneux, Professor of Physic at the University of Dublin, had little good to say of the castle when he visited Kilkenny in November 1709. He wrote of it in his journal: 'It is finely situated to the River but in no other respect answerable to the character it bears. There is not one handsome or noble apartment. The Rooms are Darke and the stairs mighty ugly. In the Duchess's Close there are some fine Pictures, as also in the Gallery, which is grand enough. . . . The Gate House and new range of buildings belonging to the Castle are mighty ugly, crooked and very expensive; tho' not yet finished the gate house having already cost, as we are tould, 15 hundred pounds.'

In 1714 the Government was informed that the second Duke was in touch with Jacobite agents. He was deprived of all his offices by George I, and when he was impeached in 1715 he went to live in England. There he continued his activity in favour of the Stuarts, urging James Edward to cross to England without delay and mount a rising. For this he was attainted and fled to France. Consequently the building work at Kilkenny was again interrupted. The estate devolved on the Butlers of Kilcash; Walter Butler went to reside in Kilkenny Castle on inheriting in 1766 and his son John, who was recognized by the Irish Parliament as the seventeenth Earl of Ormonde, lived in the castle and died there in 1795.

James, his son, the nineteenth Earl, who was made Marquess of Ormonde in 1825, undertook another major remodelling of the castle. His architect was William Robertson who had brought to his attention its perilous condition. There was no shortage of money for the project; the Marquess was one of Ireland's richest landlords, and his brother, whom he succeeded, had received £216,000 from the Government in compensation for the Crown's assumption of the hereditary right to the prisage of wines. Robertson's notes of his survey of the castle and of the discoveries made while remodelling and rebuilding

have survived. While the first Duke had tried to efface the antique castle appearance, the second Marquess of the new creation and his architect wanted to recreate the romantic appearance of a castle, and their efforts were much admired at the time. The topographer William Bartlett who was at Kilkenny when work was in progress wrote that the castle was being 'modernized within and unmodernized without'. There emerged a rather grim new castle with mock battlements and machicolation, on the plan of the medieval one. The towers were built up and castellated. Other minor changes about the middle of the last century included rather awkward balconied windows on the north front, and oriel windows and a Carrara marble chimney-piece in the great picture gallery. This gallery on the east side overlooking the River Nore housed the exceptional collection of paintings.

It is sad that this collection has now been dispersed. A catalogue of 1875 listed 184 paintings in the gallery, as well as 38 in the drawing room and others in the anteroom and library. There were portraits of the Earls attributed to Zucchero and Holbein, and works of Vandyck, Coreggio, Canaletto, Solimena, Teniers, Murillo, Tintoretto and Luca Giordano, as well as the English painters Lely, Kneller and Romney. An inventory of the contents of the castle in the time of the first Duke survives, and gives an impression of taste and luxury despite the disparaging comments of Dr Molyneux, who only liked the paintings. There were fine tapestries, some of which the Duke had taken with him to France during his exile, lacquered and crystal sconces, chairs upholstered with silk brocade and figured velvet, japanned armchairs and cabinets, silk, velvet and damask hangings, looking-glasses framed in silver and ebony or gilt, a cabinet inlaid with tortoise-shell, as well as portraits, landscapes and paintings of biblical and classical subjects.

The contents of the castle were sold in 1935 when the centuries-old residential occupation of the Butlers of Ormond came to an end. In 1967 the sixth Marquess transferred the castle to the people of Kilkenny; valiant efforts are being made to repair it and make it available for use as a museum and for civic and other functions. Under the auspices of the Butler Society members of the Butler family have come from many parts of the world in recent years to meet at Butler reunions in the castle.

The medieval world seen through nineteenth-century eyes: a label-stop in the courtyard

Killeen Castle CO. MEATH

The architect Francis Johnston remodelled the ancient castle of Killeen for the eighth Earl of Fingall in the first decade of the nineteenth century. A stronghold dating from the Anglo-Norman invasion at the end of the twelfth century, Killeen like Dunsany came to the Plunkett family through the marriage of the Cusack heiress to Sir Christopher Plunkett in 1403. Their eldest son, who got Killeen, is the progenitor of the Earls of Fingall. The Barons Dunsany descend from a second son who got Dunsany.

Johnston's inventive original plan for the adaptation and enlargement of the medieval castle is preserved in the National Library of Ireland. Unfortunately it was never executed. Lord Fingall, a Catholic, also sought the advice of Thomas Wogan Browne, a prosperous merchant and amateur architect whose hand has been discerned in the design of eighteenth-century castles of other Catholic families of the Pale. Johnston's design as executed incorporated some of Browne's ideas. It is not wholly successful, for it failed to conserve in the rebuilding the romantic atmosphere of the original. The result is a good-looking Gothick castle with classical undertones, the mantle totally masking the antiquity of the core.

James Shiel was employed to make additions and embellishments to the castle for the ninth Earl of Fingall after he succeeded to the title in 1836.

The place no longer belongs to the Earls of Fingall, of whom the present and twelfth Earl will be the last, as there is no heir. Although uninhabited because the present owner resides in a chalet he has built in the park, the castle is in an excellent state of repair.

The high quality of the decorative work and attention to detail is typical of the conscientious work of the architect Francis Johnston, below *and* above right

Killua Castle CO. WESTMEATH

It is known that the core of Killua Castle, which was extensively remodelled and enlarged in the 1830s, was an eighteenth-century house. The Gothick castle was achieved in the time of Sir Thomas Chapman, second Baronet, who died in 1837. In that year it was described as his 'handsome castellated residence', and was renowned for the fine collection of paintings there. Sir Thomas also built the follies in the park, of which the most prominent is an obelisk on a hillock to commemorate Ralegh's importation of the potato to Ireland. It is dated 1810. The architect of the castle was possibly James Shiel who built Knockdrim Castle in the same county. The Chapman baronetcy is now extinct, although there were illegitimate offspring, one of which was the controversial hero Lawrence of Arabia. The property was purchased by a Mr Hackett, but when his widow died the castle, lands, furniture and paintings were sold, and the castle was set on the road to ruin. The shell stands today like a colossal folly in the folly-girt demesne.

Once renowned for its splendid contents, this castle has joined Ireland's growing number of ghostly ruins

Killyleagh Castle CO. DOWN

Above, *the romantic castle of Killyleagh within its bawn.*
Right, *a seventeenth-century entrance-gate in the bawn wall*

Sir James Hamilton from Ayrshire was one of the most enterprising and energetic of the Scots adventurers who settled in Ireland in the seventeenth century under the English scheme for the Plantation of Ulster. His extensive land grants included a valuable estate in Co. Down, formerly the property of the O'Neills. At Killyleagh there, round the core of a castle which dated from the end of the twelfth century when John de Courcy held the lands, Sir James built a new castle reminiscent of those of his native Scotland.

It is likely that he imported materials and even workmen from Scotland and England to work at Killyleagh, as he did for his other building-projects in Ulster. We can see how the castle appeared soon after its completion in a drawing of 1625. The distinctive turret capped with a conical roof now forms the south corner of the front.

Damaged by General Monk's troops in 1648, the building was not only repaired after the Civil War, it was enlarged by an extension to the main block and a tower at the north end of the front to match the existing tower at the south end. This provides a rare instance of nostalgia for the medieval in a period when classicism was the fashion.

In 1676 Henry Hamilton, second Earl of Clanbrassil, the grandson of Sir James, died without surviving issue, having, it seems, been poisoned by his wife. The estates were divided among his heirs, and Killyleagh fell to a cousin, James Hamilton of Neilsbrook. In 1683 when he died without male issue, Killyleagh was divided so meticulously between his daughter Anne and his brother Gawin that one party got the castle and the adjacent half of the front courtyard, while the other party received the townward half of the courtyard with the lands. This impractical division was the cause of a feud between Gawin's descendants in the castle and Anne's, who built a house in their half of the courtyard. The matter was only solved after almost two centuries, in 1862, when the fifth Baron Dufferin (later first Marquess of Dufferin and Ava), the eventual heir of Anne Hamilton, married Hariot Georgina, the eldest daughter of Captain Archibald Rowan Hamilton of Killyleagh Castle, the heir of Gawin Hamilton.

The castle at that date appeared as we see it today, since an ambitious project of repair, restoration and extension had been undertaken by Archibald Rowan Hamilton and his wife. Mrs Hamilton inherited £26,000 in 1848, so that, although her husband's income from land and rents had been drastically reduced by the Famine, they were able to rebuild and improve lavishly. The work was completed within a

little more than a year, by the end of 1850, and at the surprisingly moderate cost of £7,325. Under the direction of the architect Charles (later Sir Charles) Lanyon some of the old walls were repaired, others were pulled down and rebuilt, and additions were made according to the plans of Lanyon's chief designer, W. H. Lynn, in the Scots Baronial style which he was to make popular in Ulster. The corbelled machicolations, candle-snuffer roofs and crow-stepped gables are typical. The old interior was revamped and extensively panelled.

Lord Dufferin demolished the offending eighteenth-century house in his part of the bawn, and on the day of his wedding to the daughter of the castle he laid the last stone of the handsome castellated gatehouse which he had had built for his bride's family. For an annual rental of one silver rose to the Lady Dufferin, or a pair of gilt spurs to the Lord Dufferin, he ceded his part of the courtyard to the owners of the castle; and on the coming of age of his wife's brother Gawin Rowan Hamilton in 1864, Lord Dufferin presented him with the key of the gate-house.

The tribute of a rose or gilt spurs seems appropriate for Killyleagh. Despite its distinctive Scottish features and its Irish bawn it has the air of a fairy-tale castle – glamorous, aloof and romantic, like the castles of the Loire, the Rhine or the Bavarian Alps.

Killymoon Castle CO. TYRONE

A castle designed by Nash for a wealthy client. Right, the detail of a window in the garden front, uniting uncertain historicism and discreet romanticism. See Colour Plate VIII

John Nash, the celebrated architect of Regency England, also designed a few buildings in Ireland, including some parish churches and four Gothick castles, two of which are Killymoon and Lough Cutra (p. 170). Shanbally Castle, Co. Tipperary, which he built about 1812, was larger than either of these. The fourth castle, Kilwaughter, Co. Antrim, is a not very successful adaptation of an earlier house, and is now in a state of disrepair.

Killymoon is the earliest of Nash's castles in Ireland, built about 1803 before he was engaged in radically transforming parts of London by such creations as Regent's Park, Regent Street, Trafalgar Square and Carlton House Terrace, and before his work on Brighton Pavilion. It brought him other Irish commissions through the family connections of James Stewart, Member of Parliament for Co. Tyrone, the satisfied client. The Reverend John Molesworth Staples, Rector of Lissan, for whom a new rectory was built in 1807, was James Stewart's nephew; Lord Lorton who commissioned Rockingham in 1810 was a cousin.

The house at Killymoon built by James Stewart's father, William Stewart, who also built the near-by town of Cookstown about 1750, was largely destroyed by fire about 1800. The impressive castle with a fine feudal air which Nash designed to replace it is reported to have cost £80,000. The architect's flair for the picturesque is noticeable. The castle is certainly more beautiful from a distance than it is close up. The best view is from a bridge over the Ballinderry River which runs through the demesne. An imposing building, two-storeys high above a basement, it is an ingenious composition of circular, rectangular and polygonal elements of differing heights, skilfully juxtaposed. The whole building is unified by the castellation; the castellated parapets of the towers are also machicolated. Cut-stone was used for all the new construction, which includes the front. Surviving parts of the gutted earlier house were incorporated in the new one. Nash added buttresses to the old back-quarters and remodelled their windows. Another part of the old building is the library on the west front. Nash dressed it up with buttress, heraldic stained glass and a belfry so that it has a deliberately ecclesiastical appearance.

The castle was described in the *Irish Penny Journal* in 1841 as 'one of the most aristocratic residences in the province of Ulster' with state apartments consisting of 'a breakfast-parlour, dining-room, ante-room and drawing-room, all of which are of noble proportions and their woodwork of polished oak'. Nine years later, at the death, unmarried, of William Stewart of Killymoon in 1850, the property was sold. It changed hands again in this century when the father of the present owner purchased it in depressed times for, it is reported, the ridiculous sum of £200, or even, by other accounts £100. Part of the former demesne is now a golf-course.

Kinsale (Charles Fort) CO. CORK

Charles Fort was so named in honour of the reigning monarch, Charles II, by the Viceroy, the Duke of Ormonde, when he lodged there on a visit to Kinsale in the summer of 1681. The fort was then practically new. Previously known as Ringcurran Fort, it had been constructed around the old castle of Ringcurran in 1677 by the architect Sir William Robinson, then the Superintendent of Fortifications in Ireland. With the building of the new fort the old one on the opposite side of the harbour, Castlepark, subsequently renamed James Fort, lost its former importance and eventually became obsolete.

The new stone fort, roughly star-shaped, had five bastions. The largest, the Charles, on the south-east, could cover the mouth of the harbour, and with the other bastion fronting the harbour, the Devil's on the north-west, mounted one hundred brass cannon. There were three other bastions, the North, the Flagstaff, and the Cockpit. Within the remarkable outer defences was the citadel with the Governor's house.

James II kept court in Charles Fort on the day following his landing at Kinsale in March 1689, before proceeding to Cork. The Jacobite garrisons at Kinsale still held out after the King's defeat and departure, so that they were attacked by the Williamite forces. The Governor of the Fort, Sir Edward Scott, pluckily withstood the siege for ten days, but when the Williamite artillery breached the curtain wall he negotiated terms of surrender, for he saw no chance of help arriving. One thousand men marched out of the fort with their baggage, many of whom went to the defence of Limerick. The victorious Williamite commander, the Duke of Marlborough, appointed his own brother to be the new military governor of Charles Fort.

Some handsome pedimented gateways and doorways survive, but barracks, now in ruins, were erected in the fort in the nineteenth century.

The fort's sturdy bastions

Knockelly Castle CO. TIPPERARY

The most interesting feature of this castle is its bawn wall, one of the best preserved in Ireland, with low but massive turrets at the corners. Castle and bawn were probably built by the Everards of Fethard. The castle itself consists of an exceptionally tall tower-house built in the sixteenth century and centrally situated inside the spacious bawn. In 1640 the proprietor was Nicholas Everard who, according to the Civil Survey of 1654, held the 'Castle and a slate house within a bawn by descent from his ancestors'.

In time of danger cattle were driven into the bawn and the warders retreated to the tower ready to defend the castle

159

Kylemore Castle CO. GALWAY

The Benedictine congregation known in Belgium as *De Iersche Damen* – the Irish Dames – acquired Kylemore Castle (now known as Kylemore Abbey) in the hills of Connemara as a home in 1920 after their fine abbey at Ypres in Flanders was destroyed in the First World War. They successfully established a secondary school and a summer school at Kylemore and overcame the setback of a fire in 1959.

The extraordinary baronial castle was built between 1864 and 1868 for Mitchell Henry, a highly successful Manchester financier. His mother was an Ulsterwoman and he chose a bride from Ulster, Margaret Vaughan of Quilly House, Co. Down. According to their daughter the couple spent their honeymoon touring decorously through Connemara in 1850. Near Kylemore Pass where they stopped for an al fresco lunch the young Mrs Henry saw and immediately desired to own the only dwelling in sight, a little shooting lodge on a sheltered terrace which slopes to the waters of Lough Pollacappul. Miss Henry's romantic account would have it that no sooner had Margaret impulsively exclaimed 'I would love to live there' than her bridegroom negotiated with the Blake family who owned it, and purchased it with nine thousand acres of mountain, valley, glen, river and lake, and three miles of frontage on the Atlantic Ocean. The facts are, however, that Mr Henry purchased the estate in 1862, twelve years after his marriage, when his fortune was rapidly expanding and he already had an impressive residence in London, Stratheden House. He was a tycoon who did nothing by halves. He decided to build a prestigious seat on the site of the little Connemara lodge. He did so, and with its trappings it cost him one and a quarter million pounds. When the estate had to be sold in 1902 after the collapse of Mitchell Henry's financial empire, the agents advertised the 'lavish expenditure of a beneficient owner whose princely fortune transformed a once insignificant sporting lodge into one of the most stately homes at present existent in the British Isles'.

When all was balmy at Kylemore the Henrys continued their giddy social climb. Their house-parties netted not only bankers, politicians and grandees but also eminent prelates such as Cardinal Vaughan and Archbishop McHale who were not averse to the luxury and relaxation provided.

The battlemented and towered granite castle designed by James Fuller boasted four spacious halls communicating through Gothic archways. The suite of splendid reception-rooms included a drawing-room, a ballroom with a sprung floor, a dining-room, a morning-room, breakfast-room, billiard room, library and study. There were thirty-three bedrooms, of which the two best had baths fitted in their dressing-rooms. The occupants of the other thirty-one bedrooms had to make shift with the other two bathrooms of the castle. The water pressure was ensured by an elaborate system of hydrants; a hot-water-pipe system provided heating in the winter. When electricity was invented a plant costing £2,000 was installed. In addition to a model home-farm, dairy, laundry and saw-mill on the grounds there was an ornate chapel and, near the castle, a Turkish bath.

Both the Henrys are buried in a fuchsia-shaded glade on the estate. She died of fever in Cairo in 1875, he a ruined man in 1911. After his financial disaster at the end of the century Kylemore was bought at a low price by the ninth Duke of Manchester and his wife, the former Miss Zimmerman of Cincinatti, Ohio. In the eleven years of their tenure from 1902 until 1913, when the estate was mortgaged to money-lenders, they effected some unfortunate changes. The Gothic saloon was dismantled and redecorated. The ballroom was transformed into a great kitchen. It is said that this was done to satisfy the chef who was expecting to prepare a repast for King Edward VII and Queen Alexandra when they visited Connemara in 1903. However, Their Majesties only made a pause at Kylemore Castle for tea.

The fountain no longer splashes in Mr Henry's Italian pleasure gardens, but the rugged demesne, most of which was purchased by the Land Commission, is still the home of golden plovers, curlews and widgeon, partridge, pheasants, grouse, snipe and wild duck.

See Colour Plate X

Leamaneh Castle CO. CLARE

Leamaneh is a 'strong-house' built in the first half of the seventeenth century within a bawn, adjoining and communicating with a five-storey, fifteenth-century tower. The gate (which was removed and is now at Dromoland) bears an inscription recording its erection by Conor O'Brien and Maire Ni Mahon his wife in 1643. This Maire was the notorious Maire Ruadh, Red Mary, about whom dreadful tales abound. Her portrait, which is still in the possession of the Inchiquin family, shows her as a strong and determined-looking woman in a fashionable dress ornamented with a fine Renaissance jewel.

Maire was abruptly widowed when her husband was slain in a skirmish with the Parliamentarian forces in 1651. Sudden death was no stranger to Leamaneh; Conor's great grandfather Donogh O'Brien had been hanged in the old tower-house in 1582. Maire, considering the precarious position of the inheritance of her infant son, decided that the property could best be protected by her immediate marriage to a Cromwellian. The day following her husband's death she marched resolutely to Ludlow's headquarters in Limerick, picked a Cromwellian officer and wed him. Later, it is said, their connubial arrangements were

The strong-house built by the notorious 'Red Mary' and her husband Conor O'Brien in the barren hills of Clare

blighted when the Englishman made a derogatory remark about Conor. Maire instantly pitched him out of a top-floor window. Other feats attributed to her are hanging disobedient maidservants from the corbels of the castle by their hair, and keeping a blind stallion so fierce that it was the terror of the barony.

Sir Donogh O'Brien, first Baronet, the son of Conor and Maire, left Leamaneh to live at Dromoland which became the seat of the family.

161

Leap Castle CO. OFFALY

One of the best known haunted castles in Ireland. The medieval tower was gothicized in the eighteenth century, when the pointed windows were inserted. Above, one of the windows in the tower where gory murders took place

On the site of an earlier stronghold and close to a bivallate prehistoric hill-fort and near the remains of two ring-forts, a motte-and-bailey castle and other minor earthworks, the O'Carrolls, Princes of Ely, built their castle in the fourteenth century. The site that had attracted attention throughout so many centuries commands the pass from the Slieve Bloom mountains into Munster. The earliest recorded name of the place is Léim Ui Bhanáin – O'Bannon's Leap; the O'Bannons were secondary chieftains in the area, subject to the O'Carrolls. It is so mentioned in the *Annals of the Four Masters* in an account of the Earl of Kildare's unsuccessful attempt to take the castle in 1513. Three years later, according to the *Annals,* the Earl did capture the castle, and at least partly demolished it. He later accused Sir Piers Butler of having loaned the defenders of Leap some cannon to use against him at that time. The destruction cannot have been too extensive, however, because the O'Carroll was back in his seat in 1557, when it was besieged and taken by the Earl of Sussex. Internecine clan struggles plagued the O'Carrolls throughout the sixteenth century after the death of Mulrony O'Carroll in 1532. In the bitter rivalry for the chieftainship which ensued, terrible fratricidal massacres took place, brother treacherously slaying brother in the castle. At the beginning of the seventeenth century the agents of the Crown took advantage of this situation to annexe the territory of the O'Carrolls and subject it to their programme of plantation.

In 1659 the titulado of Leap and the adjacent townlands in the Barony of Ballybritt was one Jonathan Darby, gentleman. A romantic story (for which no foundation can be discovered) would have it that a daughter of the O'Carroll chieftain fell in love with an English captain named Darby who was imprisoned in her father's castle. She smuggled food to him and eventually secured his escape. As the pair were creeping out they met her brother on the narrow mural stair and the alarm was raised. Darby ran his sword through the young O'Carroll. Then he and the maiden jumped to freedom from the battlements. Having become the heiress through the death of this brother the lady brought Leap to the Darby family when she married her English captain.

The Jonathan Darby who held the place in 1659 is said to have been a Royalist. During the Civil War he is supposed to have hidden his treasure in the grounds of the castle with the help of two servants whom he subsequently murdered to prevent them revealing the hiding-place. Be this as it may, Darby served as High Sheriff for Co. Offaly in 1674 and died at Leap in 1685.

His descendants continued in possession. About the middle of the eighteenth century his great-grandson, another Jonathan Darby, remodelled the medieval castle, giving it a Gothick dressing. The work included the windows and the doorway to the old keep, which is from a design in Batty Langley's *Gothic Architecture Restored and Improved,* published 1741.

Leap has a great reputation as a haunted castle. The most persistent elemental with which it is credited is a headless sheep with an abominable stench who frequents the tower stair. It has also been described as an evil-smelling creature, half-human, half-beast. The gory events in Leap's past, the sinister discovery of human bones in a walled-up oubliette, and of hooks used for executions in an adjacent field known as 'the Hangman's Field' have all provided material for tales of supernatural manifestations in the castle. Ghosts or no, there is an undeniable eeriness about the place. It now belongs to an Australian who plans to restore it; this may dispel the ghostly incubi.

Leixlip Castle CO. KILDARE

The gracious appearance of the castle is due to the 'Gothick' improvements made to please the eighteenth-century tenants

The Danes who once ruled a Kingdom of Dublin named the spot near the meeting of the Liffey and the Rye Water *Lax-hlaup* for the marvellous salmon-leap there. The rock on which the castle is built stands a quarter of a mile up-river. The castle has changed hands many times since the lands were granted to Adam de Hereford soon after the Anglo-Norman invasion at the end of the twelfth century. The ancient cylindrical keep is of the type popular early in the thirteenth century, and may have been built either by Adam de Hereford or by the Pypard family, who were next in possession of the site and held it until Ralph Pypard surrendered it to the Crown in 1302. It was then held for nearly two hundred years for the King by a series of constables appointed to command it.

163

Above, *the library;* right, *one of the delightfully glazed windows*

Henry VII granted the castle to Gerald, eighth Earl of Kildare, on his marriage to his second wife Elizabeth St John. With the rebellion of the Silken Thomas in the next reign the Earls forfeited Leixlip; it passed back to the Crown by the Act of 1536. Subsequently it was held by lease for short periods by Matthew King of Dublin, and William Vernon. In 1569/70 it was granted to Sir Nicholas Whyte, Master of the Rolls, whose descendants remained in possession until John Whyte sold the Manor with the village to Speaker Conolly of Castletown in 1728, and the castle with its garden and outbuildings to the Speaker's nephew, the Right Honourable William Conolly, in 1731. It is not known if the Whytes had made additions to the castle in the century and a half during which they owned it, or whether the keep and the rectangular medieval building adjoining it proved sufficient for their needs.

William Conolly made his home in the castle for twenty years, until he moved with his family to Castletown after the death of the Speaker's widow in 1752. The additions to the west of the medieval building, comprising the present library-print room,

drawing-room and staircase-hall, probably date from the period of his occupancy. His wife Lady Anne was happy at Leixlip, and indeed implied that she liked it better than Castletown: 'I daresay you would like Leixlip,' she wrote to a friend in 1734, 'As to Castletown . . . I don't think the place very pleasant, though the house is really a charming one to live in.' The Conollys let the castle when they moved to Castletown. It may have been for their first tenant, Primate Stone (who took it from 1752), or their next tenant the Viceroy, Lord Townsend (who took it from 1767 to 1772), that the castle was given a face-lift. The great walls were pierced with Gothick window-openings delightfully glazed with a pattern of rectangles, diamonds and intersecting arches, after a Batty Langley design. The Primate and the Viceroy, who both used the castle mainly as a summer residence, had a predilection for the place; the Viceroy opened the demesne to the public.

A nineteenth-century tenant, the Honourable George Cavendish, 'modernised and greatly improved' the residence during his tenancy, sometime before 1837 when the topographer Samuel Lewis reported that fact. His 'modernisation' appears to have included the mock battlements, which are not visible in earlier engravings. Two other nineteenth-century tenants met untimely ends: the Baron de Robeck fell in the river and drowned while admiring the salmon-leap in 1856; the Honourable Cornwallis Maude, son and heir of the fourth Viscount Hawarden, was killed in action in 1881 at Majuba Hill in the Zulu War.

In 1914 the fifth Baron Decies purchased Leixlip Castle and demesne. Fortunately his wife, a daughter of the American railroad tycoon George Jay Gould, was prevented from implementing the structural changes she planned and started. First the War intervened, then the political changes in Ireland, and Lord Decies decided to put the place on the market. Despite its many changes of owners and tenants, the medieval core of Leixlip has not vanished under rebuilding and its delightful eighteenth-century Gothick dress has not been spoiled.

Since 1958 the owner has been the Honourable Desmond Guinness, founder and President of the Irish Georgian Society, who has done so much to preserve buildings in the country and to stimulate interest in its architectural past. His family have been associated with the village of Leixlip for over two hundred years. The castle, now furnished and decorated with flair and discrimination, is renowned for his hospitality, and is a hub of cosmopolitan social intercourse.

Limerick Castle

The Royal city-castle known as 'King John's Castle', built above the River Shannon within the city walls, has frequently been attributed to the year 1185. The source for this dating cannot be traced beyond a statement of the sixteenth-century historian who wrote (without citing his source) that King John built Limerick Castle and bridge when he came to Ireland as Prince. On the evidence of the Annals a bawn existed there by 1200, and in 1202 a castle is mentioned. There are references also to building activity in 1207, when the Bishop of Limerick complained of encroachment on Church lands, and to repairs to the castle in 1216.

The plan of the castle is one favoured by the Anglo-Normans early in the thirteenth-century – a roughly rectangular ward surrounded by a curtain wall and defended by cylindrical towers at the angles. In fact, the plan of Limerick Castle is more exactly a pentagon because of a bend on the north wall, but a tall cylindrical tower with massive walls stood at each of the four main angles. Two strong D-shaped towers flanked the entrance on the north side, which was further protected by a portcullis and a drawbridge. The tower at the south-east corner was taken down to

King John's castle on the Shannon, and below, *the curtain wall and a medieval tower which was lowered to accommodate heavy artillery*

make place for a projecting bulwark, built on that side in 1611, and the eastern curtain wall has gone. The three remaining towers were lowered and vaulted internally to allow their use with heavy artillery. The tower at the north-west corner near the gate of the bridge, being the most important, was taller than the others.

Constables were appointed by the King to hold the castle in his name. An uninterrupted line of incumbents held this office from the appointment of Godfrey de Rupe or Roche in 1216 until the death of Viscount Gort in 1842. He was the constable in 1809 when an Act of Parliament was passed to abolish the office, effective at the death of the then incumbent. This continuity of office does not mean, however, that the castle had an unchequered history.

In 1332 when followers of the Earls of Desmond were imprisoned in the castle, they managed to murder the constable and take possession of the place. The citizens of Limerick then overran the castle and retook it, putting the men of Desmond to death there.

In 1585 the castle was reported to be in a state of disrepair. Some needed repairs were carried out about 1600 under the direction of the Lord President of

Munster, Sir George Carew. He pointed out the necessity of demolishing a part of the town adjacent to the castle in order to strengthen it adequately. These recommendations were carried out by Sir Josias Bodley, who reported their completion to Carew in 1611. In a plan in *Pacata Hibernia* drawn about that year, his improvements can be seen as he described them, principally the new bastion able to accommodate 'five or six pieces of ordnance', the moat and the drawbridge. Bodley also strengthened the bases of the towers which had been undermined by water. In the plan the twin turrets of the gate-house are shown with tall conical roofs. Against the wall on the river side a long, two-storey building is marked as a storehouse. This building was probably one of Carew's improvements.

In 1642 Captain George Courtenay with a garrison consisting of sixty of his own men, twenty-eight warders and about a hundred others, defended the castle against a strong force of Irish who had risen in rebellion. We know the day-to-day details of this siege from the diary of one of the besieged English Royalists which is preserved in Trinity College, Dublin. The Irish threw a boom of tree-trunks linked with iron across the Shannon to prevent provisions arriving by the water-gate. Then they bombarded the castle from the cathedral, ignited mines and breached the wall. The garrison was obliged to surrender. Many men of rank were among the rebels, including Lords Muskerry, Roche and Castleconnell, and the Mayor of Limerick. The insurgents later used a 32-pounder cannon captured at Limerick to reduce most of the other castles in the county.

In 1651 the Irish were forced to surrender Limerick Castle to the Parliamentary general Ireton. He had bombarded it from the foot of Thomond Bridge, and as soon as a breach was made, sent twenty dragoons in armour rushing in, followed by infantry.

Again in 1691 the castle was the scene of dramatic events when it was surrendered by the Jacobite hero Patrick Sarsfield to the Williamites, on terms which they later did not honour.

The present appearance of the castle is disimproved by houses built in the former ward, in which there was also a barracks in the eighteenth and nineteenth centuries.

Lismore Castle CO. WATERFORD

Top, *the view from the ducal castle to the gate-lodge;* above, *the fine carving of a chimney-piece in the billiard room, shamrocks with the crest of the Cavendish family, Dukes of Devonshire, a serpent nowed.* Right, *the view over the Blackwater. See Colour Plate XI*

The glamorous ducal seat of Lismore stands on the site of a castle founded, according to Giraldus Cambrensis, by the future King John when he came to Ireland in 1185. The site is at a strategic point – a crossing of the Blackwater River, and in addition had been an important ecclesiastical centre for hundreds of years. This first castle was sacked in 1189 but was retrieved by the Crown, who granted it to the bishop. In the reign of Henry III the bishop filed a complaint to the King that the Justiciary had seized his castle at Lismore while he was absent in England on state business. Lismore continued as an episcopal residence until 1589 when Myler Magrath, the rascally Archbishop of Cashel who was also Bishop of Waterford and Lismore, granted it to Sir Walter Ralegh at a rent of £13.6s.8d.

Ralegh sold the property in 1602 to another famous adventurer, Richard Boyle, later Earl of Cork, who had arrived in Ireland with only his decent clothes, a ring, a bracelet and a few pounds. At first Boyle lived in a house in Youghal where Ralegh had also resided when he visited his Irish estates, for the old castle was in a ruinous condition. From about 1610, however, Boyle, who was a passionate builder and colonizer, began work at Lismore Castle. His account books and diaries show that he followed the improvements closely, delighting even in the minutiae of the work which went on for several years. In 1614 he recorded the engagement of a stone-cutter to 'make and carve four arms and crests with the corners in freestone, one at my gallery window, one at my schoolhouse, one at my almshouse and another at my house at Lismore for £7 10 shillings, with meat, drink, and lodging at Lismore.' The castle staircase was put 'into colours', and in 1622 a plasterer was employed to 'ceil with fret work my study, my bedchamber, and the nursery at Lismore and to wash them with Spanish white'. The gardens were walled and landscaped. Inventories indicate that the castle was opulently furnished. The drawing-room walls were hung with tapestries, and throughout there were rich hangings of embroidered silk and velvet, an opulence in keeping with the owner's title of Earl of Cork, granted in 1620. His wife used a silver chamber-pot on which she once gashed her knee when her bedstaff broke as she was clambering out of the gilded bedstead. Their son Robert Boyle, the celebrated philosopher, remembered as the father of modern chemistry, was born in Lismore Castle in 1626. Another son, Lord Broghill, a prominent supporter of the Commonwealth, found himself defending the castle against a force of five thousand Irish.

The 'Great Earl's' almshouse survives in Youghal, but most of his building work at Lismore has vanished, the most substantial remainder being the garden walls which have not been changed. The castle was badly damaged when it was assaulted and taken by the Confederates in 1645, and although the second Earl had it patched up, he and his successors, who were more usually known by their additional title of Burlington, lived principally in England, showing scant interest in the Irish estates which were the main source of their wealth. Richard, fourth Earl of Cork and third Earl of Burlington, was an enthusiastic patron of the arts with a consuming interest in architecture, but it seems that he never even contemplated building in Ireland. On his death in 1753 the Burlington earldom became extinct, the Cork title devolved on a kinsman, and Lismore went to his only surviving daughter, Charlotte, wife of the fourth Duke of Devonshire.

The fifth Duke of Devonshire began to take more interest in his Irish inheritance than his maternal forbears had done for a long time. He built the bridge across the Blackwater at Lismore in 1775. The great, many-gabled Jacobean mansion with tall chimneys which had been built by the Great Earl on to the medieval castle appears in an engraving of a fine drawing by Anthony Chearnley in Smith's *The Antient and Present State of the County and City of Waterford*, published in 1746. Smith remarked on the 'great room' of the castle, with its 'great window' immediately above a precipice and overlooking the river. In 1786 the place was described as a 'venerable Ruin', and it does look derelict in a painting done by Thomas Sautelle Roberts at the end of the century.

As soon as he succeeded to the title and estates in 1811 at the age of twenty-one, the sixth Duke, who never married, decided to restore the castle, and immediately engaged William Atkinson for the project. Atkinson had studied under Wyatt and published a book on the Picturesque style in architecture. His plans largely followed the walls of the old building around the four sides of a square courtyard. His two drawing-rooms have survived practically unchanged. The main drawing-room on the north side replaced the original 'great room' with the 'great window'. The castle owes its present appearance, however, more to a revamping put in hand by the sixth Duke at the end of his life. In the vanguard of fashion as a young man, when he installed a billiard table in the hall at Lismore about 1812, at sixty the Duke was an enthusiastic admirer of the Gothic Revival. In the eight years before his death in January 1858 he made many changes at Lismore, employing as architect Joseph Paxton, the designer of the Crystal Palace. Furnishings were provided by John G. Crace and Son of London, the leading makers of Gothic Revival furniture. The robust battlements of Lismore's skyline are Paxton's work. To build them he imported stone ready-cut from England.

The 'banqueting-hall' which was used as a ballroom was designed by Pugin. The great architect, thinking back to the days of the pre-Reformation bishops who celebrated mass in the chapel on the site, gave the hall a full-blown ecclesiastical treatment. The

choir-stalls by Crace and the window with stained glass and tracery are reminiscent of a church. In Pugin's elaborate mantel in the ballroom, however, can be discerned the emerging trend of Celtic Revival. The words *Cead Mile Failte* are worked into the design.

Lismore Castle is still the property of the Dukes of Devonshire. The present and eleventh Duke maintains it splendidly. He and the Duchess use it as their residence when they are in Ireland.

Lough Cutra Castle

CO. GALWAY

Colonel Charles Vereker won fame in Government circles with his defeat of the French force which attempted an invasion at Killala Bay in 1798. He was offered a peerage as a reward but refused it, as it would have entailed voting in favour of the Union of which he was a bitter opponent. In 1810 he received the gift of the estate of Lough Cutra, then invariably written Lough Cooter, from his uncle Lord Kiltartan, later Lord Gort, whose heir he was. Having decided to build a residence in keeping with the viscountcy he expected to inherit, in the following year he commissioned the London architect John Nash to design a castle for him. The site he chose, well above the Lough, commands marvellous views. Nash's drawings of the front elevation survive, signed by him and dated October 1811. Nash massed circular and octagonal towers of differing heights to each side of a low, two-storey, double-pile, three-bay, rectangular central block. The whole building is crenellated. The construction of Lough Cutra was supervised by the efficient brothers James and George Richard Pain, pupils of Nash, whom he sent there to take charge. Nash has no great reputation for the quality of his building-work, but due to the knowledge and vigilance of the Pains Lough Cutra was superbly built. For the Pain brothers the commission was a formidable beginning to the extensive and lucrative practice they achieved in Ireland, where they later settled and built churches, civic buildings and country houses large and small.

The second Viscount Gort lived principally at Lough Cutra, where he planted the demesne and laid out the gardens, spending an immense amount of his fortune on the castle and grounds. He was a popular landlord. His uncle had given land on which the Church of Ireland parish church was built; the second Viscount gave land for the building of a Catholic

Designed by Nash and executed by the brothers Pain, the castle is well situated above the lough. Above, *the handsome chimney-piece in the octagonal library*

chapel and presented it with a handsome painting for the altar. His son, who inherited the estate and title, came near to bankruptcy. Sensible of the suffering of the masses during the Famine, he made generous donations to charities and declined to exact rents from his tenants during the worst years. In consequence he was obliged to sell Lough Cutra in 1851. The Sisters of Loreto who purchased the place found they had taken on more than they could handle. Three years later, in

1854, they sold it to the first Viscount Gough, a Limerick man who had been rewarded with a peerage for his brilliant service as a military commander. Lord Gough added the clock-tower and employed Crace and Son of London to refurbish the interior. Nash's interior, which, unlike most of his work, was devoid of classical detail, did not therefore remain intact. In honour of the owner's military career Crace used battle trophies and emblems as well as mottoes in Latin for the decorations carried out in the late 1850s. One wallpaper, by Cole, in the octagonal library, has the Viscount's coronet and cypher entangled with battle-honours and Union Jacks.

The third Viscount Gough made heavy, graceless additions to the castle after succeeding to the title in 1895. A century after his great-grandfather had been obliged to sell Lough Cutra, the seventh Viscount Gort bought it back. He gave the property to his grand-niece, a grand-daughter of Field Marshal the sixth Viscount Gort. She undertook an extensive and very costly programme of restoration to save the house, which had by then been uninhabited for about forty years. In the course of the restoration the third Viscount Gough's unhappy extensions were demolished. The castle is now the Irish residence of an appreciative owner, Mr Timothy Gwyn-Jones.

Luttrellstown Castle CO. DUBLIN

The garden front. The castle is now one of the most splendidly furnished in the country

The Luttrells who gave their name to the townland and castle beside the River Liffey at Clonsilla were one of the important families of the Pale in the late medieval period (eventually raised to the peerage as Earls of Carhampton). It is difficult to identify their castle in the agglomeration of battlemented and turretted Gothick building, mostly dating from the last decade of the eighteenth century and the first decade of the nineteenth. The thick walls of the north-east segment of the present building indicate the antique origin of that part. The old castle was, however, a large one, indeed one of the largest in the county; when Thomas Luttrell was taxed in 1664 for twelve hearths, only Rathfarnham Castle and Finglas boasted more.

As the Luttrells' fortune dwindled in the eighteenth century, that of Luke White soared. A new millionaire with an immense amount of money to spend by the end of the century, White, who had made his fortune in the giddy and fashionable lottery business, decided to acquire a grand residence. He bought the castle and lands of Luttrellstown for £180,000 and then spent lavishly on additions and improvements. To him the castle principally owes its present form, and much of its elegant interior ornamentation like the exquisite stucco of the ballroom. The park which was much admired by nineteenth-century visitors was most probably greatly improved if not laid out by Luke White.

In this century the castle was fortunate in falling into the hands of another rich and discriminating chatelain, the Honourable Mrs Brinsley Plunket, a member of the Guinness family, who was given the castle by her father as a wedding present in 1927. In her time the floor was laid in the delightful Gothick entrance-hall, a fine chimney-piece was inserted in the ballroom, a painted ceiling salvaged from a house in England was put up in the staircase-hall, and a *grisaille* room was arranged with a series of panels representing Irish trade and commerce, executed in 1788 by Peter de Gree and formerly at Collon House, Co. Louth. Elegant and magnificent furniture, tapestries and paintings combine to make Luttrellstown one of the most distinguished residences in Ireland.

Malahide Castle CO. DUBLIN

The lordship, lands and harbour of Malahide were granted to Richard Talbot by King Henry II in 1174, shortly after the invasion of Ireland, and the property remained in the possession of his descendants in the male line for the following eight hundred years. During those years Talbot possession was only once interrupted: John Talbot was evicted by Cromwell for his part in the Rebellion of 1641 and banished to Connaught, whereupon the castle with five hundred acres was granted on lease in 1653 to the regicide Miles Corbet. At the Restoration Corbet was executed and John Talbot reinstalled in his inheritance. At last, however, the Honourable Rose Maud Talbot, sister of the seventh Baron Talbot de Malahide, who had died unmarried, disposed of the castle to the Government, and most of its marvellous contents were sold at auction in 1976 and dispersed. Thus ended an unusually long association of one family with a baronial estate. Now, although there are heirs to the title, no Talbot will be living at Malahide Castle.

Eight centuries of association with one family, the Talbots, ended when the last owner emigrated to Australia in 1976. See Colour Plate XII

Though the present building incorporates substantial parts of the medieval castle, it owes its appearance mainly to rebuilding in the seventeenth and eighteenth centuries, and to alterations in the nineteenth century. The great hall still retains a medieval aspect despite the replacement timber roof and nineteenth-century minstrels' gallery. The Talbots adhered to the Roman Catholic faith until 1779, and the carving in the exquisitely panelled Oak Room suggests that this was used as their chapel. Over the mantelpiece is a Coronation of the Virgin, of Flemish origin; six panels on one wall depict Old Testament stories. The drawing rooms on the west side of the house with delightful Rococo plasterwork were built in the 1760s by Richard Talbot and his wife Margaret O'Reilly, later created Baroness Talbot de Malahide. They replaced a series of smaller and lower tapestry-hung chambers which were destroyed when the west side of the castle was gutted by fire. At the same time the old outside walls were built up and circular turrets were added at the north-west and south-west corners.

These contain delightful little turret rooms with ogee Gothick windows, communicating with the two large reception-rooms. The arrangement is similar to that at Margaret's family home, Ballinlough Castle in Co. Westmeath, and illustrates an interesting phase in eighteenth-century Revival fashion.

The seventh Baron Talbot de Malahide who succeeded to the title and estate on the death of a cousin in 1948 was an enthusiastic and knowledgeable gardener. At his death in 1973 he left his ancestral castle the delightful legacy of magnificent gardens planted with rare and interesting specimens, collected from many parts of the southern hemisphere. There are now more than 4,500 different species and cultivars to admire in the gardens, which cover fifteen acres, five of which comprise the walled garden with a sunken lily pool.

Mallow Castle CO. CORK

A fortress, it seems, had been built on the Blackwater River at Mallow at the end of the twelfth century, but in 1282 the Desmond Geraldines became possessed of the place, and built for themselves a castle which remained in their tenure until the Palatinate was forfeited and confiscated after the Desmond Rebellion. During the fighting of the rebellion the castle was badly damaged, in particular the five-storey tower, detached hall with barbican, and two small inner wards, as well as the bridge over the Blackwater which it guarded. The Seignory of Mallow, which included this damaged castle and six thousand acres, was granted in 1588 to Sir Thomas Norreys, who then held office as vice-president to his brother Sir John, whom he later succeeded in 1597 as Lord President of Munster.

Sir Thomas came to live at Mallow, and it appears that before his death in 1599 he had at least begun the building of the important fortified house whose shell survives. The Commissioners who surveyed the Plantation of Munster reported in 1622 that: 'There was built at Mallow by Sir Thomas Norris, a goodly strong and sumptuous house, upon the ruins of the old castle, with a bawn to it about 120 foot square and 18 foot in height and many convenient houses of office.' From this one might conclude that the house and offices were completed by Sir Thomas in his lifetime,

The ruins of Lord President Norrey's 'goodly strong and sumptuous house'

but the comments of earlier visitors suggest that it was unfinished at his death. The Attorney-General who lodged there with the widowed Lady Norreys in 1606 described it as 'a well-built house, and stands by a fair river in a fruitful soil, but it is yet much unrepaired and bears many marks of the late rebellion'. The estate was inherited at Sir Thomas's death by his infant daughter and only child Elizabeth, named for her godmother, the Queen, whose gift to her of two white harts are claimed to be the origin of the unusual white-grained herd at Mallow.

While still a minor, Elizabeth Norreys married Sir John Jephson, and in 1612 the grant of the Manor was confirmed to her, along with further properties, jointly with her husband. It appears, therefore, that the last remains of the damaged castle were demolished and the new house completed, according to the original design, by the Jephsons between about 1607 and 1622 when the Commissioners saw it. There is some evidence in the building-work itself that the house was built in two sections: the northern half first (probably before 1599), and the southern half, butted against it, not long after. What appear to be parts of the heavy foundations of the Desmond castle have been discerned in the southern part near the cross-wall. It is probable that in 1606 much more of the ruins still stood adjoining the new construction.

The house is a long, single-pile rectangle, four storeys in height, designed with high gables and chimneys and mullioned windows with chamfered hood-mouldings. There are firing holes under some of the upper windows. The defence rested, however, mainly in the polygonal turrets at the north-west and south-west corners; both communicated with the house, and the northern one, which contained a stair, once had set in its upper storey the clock now on Mallow clock-house. The front entrance of the house was further protected by an angular, turret-like projecting wing in the centre, before the door. Another larger wing projecting at the centre-rear contained the main stair.

The Jephson family, lineal descendants of Sir John Jephson and Elizabeth Norreys, still retain the core of the estate and reside at Mallow. The castle was badly damaged in the fighting between Jacobites and Williamites in 1690, so that the family was obliged to abandon it. They first moved into the stable buildings, which were made habitable, and eventually, after a projected restoration of the old castle in 1829 was deemed impracticable, the present family residence was built there, mainly in the 1830s, in the style of a Tudor Revival manor house.

Maynooth is now famous for its co-educational theological college, founded at the end of the eighteenth century for the higher education of the Irish Catholic priesthood. In medieval times Maynooth was dominated by the castle of the great Earls of Kildare. For more than two hundred years, from the early fourteenth to the sixteenth century, it was their chief residence.

A castle was built at Maynooth soon after the Anglo-Norman invasion at the end of the twelfth century. In 1328 there is mention of a stone castle with two gates, one to the town and the other to the gardens. The sixth Earl of Kildare enlarged and rebuilt the castle in 1426. In 1535 it was besieged in the course of the rebellion of the Silken Thomas. His garrison was massacred although they surrendered unconditionally, because, as the Lord Deputy wrote to Henry VIII: 'moost of theym beyng gunners, at some other tyme wold semblablie elliswhear aid your traitors, and be example and meane to others to doo lykewise, we all thought expedient and requisite, that they shulde be put to execution, for the dread and example of others'.

The 'Great Earl' of Cork, who married his daughter to the fifteenth Earl of Kildare, repaired part of the castle and built a new house for the couple between 1630 and 1634. By the end of the seventeenth century, however, all was derelict. Now only the ruined keep and gate-house survive.

The ancient gate of the medieval seat of the powerful Earls of Kildare, where the Silken Thomas's garrison was butchered

Pynnar, in his survey of Ulster made in 1619–20, described the castle at Monea as 'standing 50 feet in height and surrounded by a wall 9 feet in height and 300 feet in circuit'. Much of this bawn wall is still intact. Indeed, Monea is probably the best preserved of all the castles of the Plantation of Ulster.

At the time of Pynnar's visit the castle had newly been built by the Rector of Devenish, the Reverend Malcolm Hamilton, who was subsequently promoted and consecrated Archbishop of Cashel in 1623. Besides the distinctive Scottish corbelling it has another imported feature: the two round towers spanned by a lofty arch which guarded the entrance are corbelled out at their summit to carry rectangular heads – square chambers set diagonally above the towers, their projecting corners supported by courses of corbelling. The purpose of this ingenious means of lateral expansion would seem to be more decorative than functional. Indeed the effect is made more elaborate by the crow-stepped gables of the chambers above the towers. The same device can be seen in Scotland at the castle of Claypotts in Angus which remains complete and unchanged since it was built in the late sixteenth century.

Monea, which once had a slated roof, is built of a hard carboniferous limestone, and its walls are still stout. The principal rooms, as usual, were on the first floor, lit by large windows without mullions and with window-seats in the embrasures.

The Irish insurgents seized the castle in the Rebellion of 1641, but it was retaken by the forces of the Crown and used as a residence in 1688 by Gustavus Hamilton, then Governor of Enniskillen, and later Brigadier General of King William III's armies, Privy Councillor and first Viscount Boyne. It lay in ruins for many years after a fire in the eighteenth century. In the last century a weird old woman named Bell M'Cabe, locally reputed to be a witch, was a squatter in the vault at the base of one of the towers.

A substantial castle of the Ulster Plantation, built in the style of his native land by an undertaker from Scotland

Monkstown Castle CO. DUBLIN

Most of the present remains of the castle of Monkstown date from the fifteenth or sixteenth century, when it was built on the site of an earlier castle owned by the monks of the important Cistercian Abbey of St Mary in Dublin, from whom the place gets its name. The monks had lost their castle with the rest of the abbatial estates when they were surrendered to the Crown in 1539 by William Laundie, the last abbot. The list of their possessions included five 'fortalices' or castles.

Subsequently the place changed hands many times. In the seventeenth century the Cromwellian general Ludlow resided there: 'Edmond Lodlowe Esq' is shown as the titulado of 'Mounk towne' in 1659. Later in the century the castle was the residence of Archbishop Boyle. He was followed by a series of undistinguished tenants. A new Monkstown Castle was erected near the ruins of the old in the nineteenth century. It was described as a 'modern house' in 1837, when it was the residence of Lynden Bolton Esq.

Later in the nineteenth century, when antiquarian fever was raging, the old buildings were enthusiastically manhandled and mutilated. The fifteenth- or sixteenth-century gate-house was left more or less intact, but the bawn, of which the castle forms a part, was rebuilt. The castle is now a National Monument.

The castle, the restored bawn wall, and the original gate-house

Narrow Water Castle CO. DOWN

The old tower-house beside the main road from Newry to Warrenpoint was built in the 1560s: in 1568 the warder John Sancky was paid a Government subsidy of £361.4s.2d for building it. The site was an important one because the Newry River narrows here, allowing a ferry-crossing which cuts out a considerable journey by land. The tower is described in 1570 as 'one new castle within the which are two chambers and a cellar and a hall covered with straw and a stable nigh unto the said castles . . . and nine cottages covered with earth within the precinct'.

The Magennises of Iveagh acquired Narrow Water by 1580, and held it until they forfeited it with the rest of their estates in the next century. Joseph Dean of Crumlin, Co. Dublin, then obtained it, and sold it in 1670 to Francis Hall who was later High Sheriff of the county. It is uncertain whether the Halls ever lived in the old tower-house, for they built a house which they called Mount Hall near by, on higher ground. They may have occupied it for a period while their new house was being completed and before Francis Hall's death in 1706.

fireplace and deep window embrasures. There are small chambers in the thickness of the wall at three of its corners; the fourth corner is occupied by the stair. At roof-level a rectangular tower rises to a third storey which contained one room; entrance to it was from the wall-walk behind the battlemented parapet. The gabled roof over the tower contained attic rooms.

The late seventeenth-century house built by the Halls up on the hill now forms the long, two-storey staff-wing of their nineteenth-century castle. Some of its original features are discernible at the rear. Roger Hall, High Sheriff of County Down in 1816, built the family's Tudor Revival mansion in the 1830s. The topographer Samuel Lewis described it in 1837 as 'a very fine edifice in the Elizabethan style built of hewn granite raised from a quarry on the estate'. It has been ascribed to the English architect Edward Blore who built Crom Castle in Co. Fermanagh for the Earl of Erne between 1830 and 1837. While it does not appear in a list of major works by Blore prepared from his account books in Cambridge University Library by Marc Girouard, this may be because the list excludes alterations and enlargements, even substantial ones. The new castle has a splendid interior with a beautiful stair and some high-quality plasterwork and panelling. Some of the furniture and an elaborately carved mantel are the work of Curran, a craftsman from Lisburn.

Mr Roger Hall, the present owner of the estate, lives in the 'new' castle with his family. In 1956 he handed over the old castle to the Government of Northern Ireland. It is classified as an Ancient Monument and is in State care.

Left, the sixteenth-century tower commanding the crossing of the Newry River; below, the garden front of the Tudor Revival castle built in the 1830s

The tower is built of rubble-stone with chiselled granite quoins and some dressings of sandstone, and it stands within a walled bawn. It is battered, not from the base, but from a few feet above ground-level. It has three storeys and attics. A machicolation on the west front carried by roof-level corbels protected the entrance on the ground floor; a garderobe with an external chute is in the south-west corner. This first-floor chamber was probably a guardroom where soldiers lived and slept when the castle was garrisoned. On the second floor is a chamber with a

XII Malahide Castle CO. DUBLIN

Parts of Malahide are medieval, but rebuilding went on through the centuries. The Gothick windows are a charming eighteenth-century conceit. *See* p. 173.

XIII Newtown Castle CO. CLARE

An unusual cylindrical tower-house, built in the sixteenth century when rectangular tower-houses were the norm.

XIV Nenagh Castle CO. TIPPERARY

The massive early thirteenth-century keep to which a top storey and battlements were added in the nineteenth century by an enthusiastic local antiquarian.

XV Slane Castle CO. MEATH

An elegant Revival castle for which designs were made by Wyatt, Capability Brown, Gandon and Francis Johnston. *See* p. 196.

Parke's Castle CO. LEITRIM

*A sixteenth-century Planter's castle with a stout bawn wall
built on the site of a fortress of the chiefs of Breffny*

At Newtown, on the shore of Lough Gill, the O'Rorkes, rulers of Breffny, had one of their strongholds. This was the castle where in 1588 Sir Brian O'Rorke entertained Francisco de Cuellar, the shipwrecked Spanish Armada officer who later defended Rossclogher Castle. In his account of his experiences in Ireland Captain de Cuellar writes of the chief, who was a bitter enemy of the English and the epitome of a princely Irish leader of the old order: 'Although this chief is a savage, he is a good Christian and an enemy of the heretics and is always at war with them.'

On one occasion Sir Richard Bingham set out secretly at night with a footband to surprise O'Rorke in his castle and take him prisoner. O'Rorke, however, warned by some of his henchmen who had espied the Governor and his men, leapt from the castle into a boat below and escaped across the lough to the fastness of the woods. He was finally delivered to the authorities in Scotland where he had mistakenly gone to seek help, arraigned for high treason, indicted and executed on the gallows in London in 1591.

The estates of the chief were confiscated and redistributed. In 1659 the titulado of Newtown was Robert Parker Esq. It is evidently from this Parker or his family that the seventeenth-century Plantation castle built on the site of O'Rorke's stronghold got its name 'Park's' or 'Parke's'. It has three storeys and mullioned windows, and forms part of one side of a spacious pentagonal bawn. Incorporated into it is one of the two circular flanking turrets which protected corners of the bawn. Another side of the bawn wall overlooks the lake. The entrance to the bawn is through a passageway in the ground floor of the house.

The castle was sturdily built and the walls are well preserved. It is not known when it was abandoned as a residence. It appears to have been long deserted in 1837 when Samuel Lewis described it as 'the ruins of a fine old castle'. It is now a National Monument. In the course of excavation and repairs by the Office of Works vestiges of the earlier castle have been discovered, but it is still not clear to what extent the plan of the Planter's mansion and bawn followed that of the earlier Irish stronghold.

Portumna Castle CO. GALWAY

Portumna Castle, built near the shore of the northern extremity of Lough Derg in the reign of James I, was almost certainly without equal in Ireland at the time in style, grandeur and distinction, outshining Archbishop Loftus's Rathfarnham, Donogh MacCarthy's Kanturk, Sir Arthur Chichester's Joymount at Carrickfergus and Sir Toby Caulfield's Charlemont, which Pynnar described as the fairest building he had seen.

The elegance of Portumna can be attributed to the taste, experience and wealth of its builder, Richard Burke, fourth Earl of Clanrickarde, Lord President of Connaught, scion of a fiery clan of Norman origin which had held sway over great parts of Connaught for four centuries. By the time of the fourth Earl the unruly and powerful Burkes had been cajoled into loyalty to the Crown, and he was brought up partly in England to be anglicized, and educated at Oxford. He fought with the English at Kinsale where he was knighted on the field of battle by the victorious Lord Deputy, and, soon after, married the daughter and heiress of that rich and redoubtable servant of the Crown, Sir Francis Walsingham, whose intelligence brought Mary Queen of Scots to the scaffold. The new Countess had been twice widowed; her previous husbands were both eminent Elizabethans, the first Sir Philip Sidney, the second, the ill-fated Earl of Essex who after his unfortunate Irish campaign was beheaded for treason in 1601. The Earl and Countess lived in England in the mansion they built at Tonbridge in Kent in 1613, and there is no evidence that they ever lived in, or even saw, their splendid Irish seat.

Portumna was one of the first, if not the first, building in the country to admit some of the Renaissance refinements already common in Italy and France for over a century, but which took so long to filter through to Ireland and find lodgement there. Even the shell of this great mansion (for the interior was accidentally destroyed by a fire in 1826) conveys an impression of alien splendour. Although the details of Portumna can be found in other Jacobean buildings, both in Ireland and in England, the overall effect is unique, and has a curiously Continental air.

Of necessity in trouble-prone Connaught, the house was provided with elements of defence, such as the firing holes round the doors and a machicoulis above the main entrance. But the Earl built what was essentially a residence rather than a fortress, a place conceived for pleasure and gracious living, in contrast to the defensible shelters oblivious to comfort or elegance which were then the homes of most of the

The splendid seventeenth-century castle, of a refinement rare in Ireland at the period, with its regularly placed windows and curved gables

187

Irish lords. The traditional name 'strong-house' is the best epithet for Portumna, since it describes just what it was. It stands three storeys above cellars, a double-pile of six bays with delightfully symmetrical fenestration, two- and three-mullion windows regularly placed, and a distinctive crenellated parapet relieved with attractive curvilinear gables. Massive supporting walls set ten feet apart divided the two piles of the house longitudinally, creating a crossing corridor, from each end of which dark oak stairs rose to the upper floors. The ground plan is a favoured one: a rectangle with flanking towers at each corner. From the accounts of nineteenth-century visitors it is known that the interior was richly decorated with plasterwork friezes, carved armorial bearings and handsome panelling, but only the barest fragments of the decorative plasterwork remain.

The fine Jacobean doorcase before its recent restoration. Note the firing holes placed at either side

The Renaissance features of the exterior of Portumna are strictly speaking limited to the fine doorcase of the front entrance and the gateway of the innermost courtyard, but the very lay-out is an expression of Renaissance ideas, for the house is set at the south end of two spacious courtyards with a magnificent axial approach through a series of gateways. It was the custom for carriages arriving along this main drive from the north to stop at the gate of the inner courtyard, rather than before the door; visitors alighted and crossed the court to the door of the castle on foot, the gentlemen bareheaded regardless of the weather.

In 1634 the unpopular Lord Deputy Strafford requisitioned Portumna in order to hold an inquisition there into the titles to lands in Connaught and the rights of the Crown to them. The Earl was vexed by this intrusion and, according to his son, the news of it hastened his death, which occurred the next year. This son, Ulick, fifth Earl of Clanrickarde, returned to Ireland and made Portumna his residence, remaining there through the troubled period of the 1641 Rising and part of the Civil War, although like his father he died in England. The Cromwellian General Ludlow besieged and took the castle, which, with the rest of the vast Clanrickarde estates, was forfeited and granted to Henry Cromwell, the Protector's son. At the Restoration the fifth Earl's widow was reinstated and returned to Portumna. In 1690 the title was held by the eighth Earl, who conformed to the Established Church but remained loyal to James II. In that year the Jacobite garrison at Portumna was besieged by the Williamite forces and surrendered; in the following year the Earl was obliged to surrender Athlone to the victorious Dutch Williamite general Ginckel. The next and ninth Earl persevered in the Jacobite cause and fought at Aughrim. Consequently he was attainted, and the castle and estates were forfeited, again to be subsequently restored to the family who continued in residence, in considerable pomp, until the fire of 1826, after which they did not attempt to repair the old castle but built a new seat in the park. This was burned in the Civil War in 1922, when the memory of the last Marquess, an unloved miser and a notoriously bad landlord, was still fresh. At his death in 1916 the ancient Clanrickarde title became extinct. The castle ruin is now a National Monument.

The castle seen from across the spacious forecourts

Rathmacknee Castle CO. WEXFORD

A bartizan protecting one of the corners of the bawn

The lands of Rathmacknee belonged to the Rosseter or Rossiter family in the fifteenth century. From its appearance the castle dates from the second half of the fifteenth century, so that it was probably built by John Rosseter, Seneschal of the Liberties of Wexford in 1451. The Rossiters survived the Reformation purges although they did not accept the new faith, but by 1659 they were out. In that year the titulado of 'Rath Mc Knee' was Thomas Hart Esq. In 1837 the topographer Samuel Lewis reported that the ancient castle, 'one of the most perfect of the numerous castles in this county', had continued inhabited until seventy years before, when its occupier had been an ancestor of H. Knox Grogan-Morgan, the then proprietor.

The castle is still in good condition and almost complete. The well-preserved curtain wall surrounds a rectangular bawn with an entrance on the east side through a pointed arch in the wall. At the north-east corner the bawn wall has a rounded turret-like bartizan projected on corbels. A rectangular bartizan protected the north-west angle. The five-storey tower with its attractive stepped-battlements stands at the south-east corner of the bawn. A pretty cottage in the bawn is inhabited.

Rockfleet Castle CO. MAYO

This neat little tower-house stands on an inlet of Clew Bay. Whether it is seen in the dappled sunlight of a summer evening against the backdrop of blue water and mountains, or stark and desolate on a winter's day when the waters are dark and white-capped, it can hardly fail to delight the viewer despite its unpretentious simplicity. The tower has four storeys and a small rectangular corner turret rising above the parapet. It was built in the sixteenth century. The principal apartment must have been on the top floor where there is a fireplace.

The castle, formerly known as Carrigahowley, an anglicization of its Irish name *Carraig an Chabhlaigh*, translated as Rockfleet, belonged to the O'Malleys. It was in the possession of the high-spirited and intrepid Granuaile or Grainne ni Mháille, Grace O'Malley, called 'the Pirate Queen' because of her redoubtable maritime adventures. The O'Malley territory of her sept included hundreds of rocky inlets and the western isles. Grace, a chief's daughter, married in turn two Connaught chiefs, O'Flaherty and Burke, and she triumphantly vanquished any pretenders to dominion of the western coast. When the Sheriff of Galway sent a large sea-borne expedition to take Rockfleet Castle, Grace routed his forces in a naval battle. After the death in 1583 of her second husband Sir Richard Burke, the Mac William Oughter, known as Richard of the Iron, she made Rockfleet her home, retiring there with 'all her own followers and one thousand head of cows and mares'. One must conclude that there were then some cabins clustered about the castle to accommodate all the lady's retainers. Widowhood did not affect Grace's penchant for the dangerous life. She was at the head of the O'Malleys when they annihilated ships of the dispersed Spanish Armada in 1588 off Clare Island at the entrance to Clew Bay, where her large vessels were kept moored. The Spanish crews were summarily dealt with. This unsavoury exploit attracted the curiosity and grateful attention of Queen Elizabeth, who received Grace at court in England. Presumably it was at Rockfleet that the Lord Howth's heir (p. 138) was kept for some of the time when he was kidnapped by Grace on her return to Mayo from England by sea.

Grace O'Malley, the intrepid chieftainess known as 'the Pirate Queen', conducted naval forays from this remote tower-house

Roodstown Castle CO. LOUTH

An unadorned fifteenth-century fortress; an efficient murder-hole protects the entrance

The four-storey tower now stands alone in a field; its outer defences have vanished. The tower has the usual features of its period – a vaulted ground floor, a murder-hole in the entrance-passage, a well-defended parapet and a wall-walk – but it is unusual in having two projecting turrets rising from the ground to the full height of the tower. One of these angle-turrets contains the spiral stair leading to all floors and the roof; the other contains a garde-robe and some small chambers. The windows of the tower are finely made. One in particular, which lights the first-floor apartment, deserves attention: it is larger than the others and has twin lights with a transom, each light having a well-shaped trefoiled ogee head.

Rossclogher Castle

CO. LEITRIM

In a country where a pastoral people lived in almost constant danger of attack by human and animal marauders, a lake-dwelling which offered safety from both was a popular form of habitation from the Iron Age until late medieval times. A dwelling of timber, wattle or mud was built on a promontory almost entirely surrounded by water, on a natural islet, or on a *crannóg,* an artificial substructure of stones constructed in a lake or on its marshy shore. Access to the *crannóg* would be by tortuous footpaths through the marshes, hidden beneath the surface of the water. On one such *crannóg,* a foundation of heavy stones laid in the bed of Lough Melvin about one hundred yards from the marshy shore and filled to water-level with smaller stones and earth, the M'Glannagh chiefs, who had undoubtedly used the site for centuries, built a stone castle about the beginning of the sixteenth century. It consisted then of a thick-walled cylindrical keep and a bastion. As it appears today, a creeper-clad stump rising above the reeds of a barely visible islet, it is hard to imagine Rossclogher Castle the impregnable stronghold of a daring chief, or the scene of stirring events when it was successfully defended against a huge English force by nine desperate Spanish survivors of a wrecked Armada galleon.

The M'Glannaghs, secondary chieftains subject to the O'Rorkes, ruled a small but strategically important territory on the eastern seaboard of Breffny, including a stretch of the vital coastal route from Connaught to Tyrconnel. Inland, their territory was wild and

Roodstown is one of the best preserved of the tower-houses that survive from the great number which once dotted the Pale. The Government, in order to encourage the gentlemen of County Louth to build fortifications which would help protect it from depredations and encroachments, offered in 1429 a premium of £10 to anyone building a tower. The tower had to be completed within five years, rise to a minimum height of 40 feet and have a minimum length and breadth of 20 feet by 16 feet. In 1430 the offer was extended to the other counties of the Pale. Roodstown Castle was built in the fifteenth century, and its erection may well have been due to the encouragement of the subsidy offered in 1429.

inaccessible, a country of mountains, woods, lakes and bog. The chief in the reign of Elizabeth I was an implacable enemy of the Crown, described by the Governor of Connaught as 'an arch-rebel'. At Kinlough he kept an effigy of the Queen which the people battered and reviled to express their contempt.

In September 1588 over a thousand Spaniards were drowned when their ships foundered off the Sligo coast. A few who reached Streedagh Strand managed to make their way inland. The Governor of Connaught reported that the M'Glannagh, together with the O'Rorke and others, had 'combined with the Spaniards', and that he truculently proclaimed that his kerne were 'making way for King Philip'. Reports also reached the Lord Deputy that M'Glannagh was preventing the passage of Government agents along the road from Sligo to Ballyshannon. Nine Spaniards were with the Chief when he learned of the approach of a force sent by the Lord Deputy to capture him. 'One Sunday after Mass', wrote Captain de Cuellar, one of these Spaniards, 'the chief took us on one side and with his hair over his eyes and in a furious rage told us that he could remain there no longer, that he had decided to flee with all his people, their cattle and families. . . . Since the native chieftain was so loth to leave his castle unprotected, we nine Spaniards would gladly remain in it and defend it with our lives; this we could do very well, even if twice as many more should attack it as were now approaching, because the castle was extremely strong and very difficult to storm without artillery, for it was built in the middle of a very deep lake . . . with an outlet to the sea. Even during the spring tides there was no means of entry that way, so that the castle could not be taken either from the water or from the nearest strip of land. . . . On the mainland there is a swamp, breast-deep, so that even the inhabitants can only reach it by footpaths.' The Chief supplied the Spaniards with muskets, arquebuses, stones and provisions to last several months. The Lord Deputy's troops encamped about a mile off and sounded trumpet-calls to surrender which were disdained by the Spaniards. After seventeen days, the English were obliged to abandon their siege and return to Dublin. However, later, on Good Friday of 1590, the Sheriff of Sligo captured M'Glannagh, apparently at Rossclogher. With jubilant relief the Governor reported, 'M'Glannagh's head brought in. . . . M'Glannagh ran for a loch which was near and tried to save himself by swimming, but a shot broke his arm, and a gallowglass brought him ashore. . . . He was the most barbarous creature in Ireland and had always 100 knaves about him.'

This ruined stump of a castle exemplifies the principle of the ancient crannóg *or lake-dwelling*

Roscommon Castle CO. ROSCOMMON

One hundred years after the Anglo-Norman invasion and the formal submission of the Irish chiefs to Henry II as Lord of Ireland, the Royal writ could still only be enforced in a small part of the island. In an effort to remedy this situation and establish effective control over the troublesome outlying areas the Crown embarked on a programme of castle-building in the 1270s. In the course of this initiative the Justiciar made a visitation in eastern Connaught to find a suitable site for a fortress in the cantred of Roscommon. The only spot which met his requirements happened to be on land belonging to the Augustinian priory of St Comman. This did not deter the Justiciar. Without seeking the permission of the ecclesiastical authorities he had building started. Not till twelve years later was the monastery compensated for the

loss. The Church in Roscommon was not then unused to receive short shrift from the Government. In 1275 the Dominican friars of St Mary's Roscommon complained to the King that a former Justiciar had appropriated money and goods deposited in the church by poor people, for the use of his army.

As soon as building operations began in 1269–70 the native Irish under Hugh O'Conor attacked. In 1272 and again in 1277 they demolished what had been built. These setbacks did not dishearten the English. Instead they were incited to build a stronger and more impregnable fortress. Work was in progress on this from 1280 to 1285, and continued sporadically after that for upwards of twenty years. The curtain wall which enclosed a spacious quadrangle, 162 feet by 130 feet, was under construction in 1284. Already by 1304

the two portcullises, one protecting the main gateway and one the postern gate, and three drawbridges, all needed repairs.

Despite the numerous attacks it has withstood, the alterations made in 1578 by Sir Nicholas Malby who changed the fenestration, inserting mullioned windows, and the damage caused by the Cromwellians who attacked and subsequently dismantled the castle in 1652, it remains today an impressive sight, an example of superior Anglo-Norman military architecture in the thirteenth century.

The lay-out of this keepless castle is similar to that of Harlech Castle in Wales, begun in 1283, save that Harlech has a second curtain wall enclosing an outer bailey. However, a reference to 'two outer bridges' at Roscommon in 1304 implies that it, too, had at least an outer ditch or some kind of outer fortifications. At each corner of the curtain wall, which has lost its crenellated parapet, stands a projecting D-shaped tower. These towers once had three storeys, as did the twin towers which flank the gateway on the east wall. They are rounded on the outside and rectangular inside the bailey, shaped like elongated D's. The postern gate is through a rectangular tower projecting from the west wall near the south-west corner. A symmetrical moat some distance from the curtain walls surrounded the whole castle.

The thirteenth-century bastions and some sixteenth-century buildings are the impressive remains of the castle attacked and dismantled by Cromwell in 1652

Slane Castle CO. MEATH

The Duke of Leinster tried to persuade Capability Brown to come to Ireland by offering him £1,000 as a gift on his landing, but Brown politely refused with the excuse that he had 'not yet finished England'. Although he never did come to Ireland, Brown made some designs for Slane Castle for the first Viscount (later Earl) Conyngham. The plan, unsigned, but marked 'A specimen of Capability Brown's skill in architecture' is an elevation of the stable-range with a Gothick centre-piece. It corresponds with the façade as executed. Brown's biographer, Dorothy Stroud, has conjectured that he may also have sent over designs for the splendid landscape at Slane.

Lord Conyngham had plenty of money to spend. In addition to the income from his Irish estates he had the considerable fortune of his wife Ellen, daughter and heiress of Solomon Merretto, a rich merchant and banker. This enabled him to engage other leading architects to make designs. One design, of a hall in the classical style by James Wyatt, dated 1775, is preserved at Slane.

However the Earl died in 1781, and it is not clear exactly what had been accomplished at that time. He was succeeded by special remainder, in the Barony only, by his sister's son Francis Pierpont Burton, who, as second Baron Conyngham proceeded with the rebuilding of the castle. Lord Conyngham consulted the leading architect in Dublin, James Gandon, who made sketches for a Gothick elevation in 1783. Work seems to have been started in that year. Thomas Penrose surveyed the buildings already on the site of and probably partly incorporating the medieval castle of the Flemings, Lords of Slane, who had forfeited their estates in the seventeenth century. In 1785 Lord Conyngham called back Wyatt, who had made some designs ten years earlier for his uncle, to take over the whole project. Wyatt proceeded to demolish the existing buildings, down to the basement level at the front of the house and to the first-floor level on the other sides. On these foundations, in 1785 and 1786, Wyatt built Slane Castle much as it now appears. As might be expected of an architect of Wyatt's stature, the result is impeccable. Despite its castellated towers, Slane Castle is basically a classical mansion with a Gothick dress in the best tradition of the late eighteenth century. The Irish architect Francis Johnston, Wyatt's disciple, worked at Slane with or after him. According to his own statement, Johnston finished the entrance to the castle, the hall and the staircase. The Gothick library or ballroom of the castle is superb, one of the earliest examples of interior decoration in this style in Ireland. The intricate ceiling-tracery, exquisitely wrought, somehow recalls the delicate and playful spirit of the Irish Rococo stuccodores of the preceding generation. It dates from the time of Wyatt's work, but may well have been executed under the supervision of Johnston who became proficient in such decoration, using it himself at Killeen Castle and in the Chapel Royal of Dublin Castle.

The second Baron Conyngham was succeeded in 1787 by his son, created Marquess Conyngham in 1816. The Marchioness was a favourite of the Prince Regent, who visited the Conynghams at Slane during his Regency and again after his coronation as George IV. Six bronze plaques depicting events in the life of Louis XIV are set in the walls of the hall; these gifts from George IV are a memento of his passion for Lady Conyngham. They are half of a set taken from a demolished monument to the French King (the other half is in the Louvre). The seventh and present Marquess lived at Slane Castle with his family. He has allowed it to be used for June concerts of the Festival of Music in Irish Country Houses, when its beauty and splendid furniture were greatly admired.

Below, the entrance-gates with the armorial bearings of the Marquess of Conyngham. Right, the exquisitely executed ceiling of the ballroom of the elegant Revival castle where George IV dallied with Lady Conyngham

Thomastown Castle

CO. TIPPERARY

There was a flurry of building activity in the Ormond Palatinate in the time of Charles II when the first Duke was Viceroy of Ireland. The Duchess built a classical mansion in pink brick at Dunmore near Kilkenny, thereby stimulating this activity and contributing to making brick popular as a building material. George Mathew of Thomastown was in the vanguard of fashion when he built a two-storey house in the classical style in reddish-pink brick on his Tipperary lands. His grandson, another George Mathew, considerably enlarged the house early in the eighteenth century, and laid out the formal garden and landscape with ponds and terraces. Until 1972 at least the outline of the beds and shrubberies could be seen, but now the area has been levelled.

The Mathews, in due course, moved up into the ranks of the peerage as Earls of Llandaff. In 1812 when the second Earl succeeded to the title, castle-building was fashionable, and he decided to transform his mansion into a Tudor castle. To do this he engaged the architect Richard Morrison. The old mansion all but vanished in and under the vast new castle, a romantically conceived amalgamation of Gothic and Tudor styles. The old mansion had an open arcade at the front. The arches of this were gothicized and

The picturesque silhouette of this Tudor Revival castle is a precursor of the more vigorous roving skylines of the Victorians later in the century

glazed to create a hall, in the centre back wall of which a chimney-piece was installed with stucco crocketing. Most of the main rooms of the old mansion with the exception of the drawing-room were also gothicized. The whole building was refaced and liberally peppered with battlemented towers and turrets of various shapes. Two tall slender towers with fantastic crenellations and fanciful, bogus-looking smaller turrets rising like spirelets from their roofs, were built to flank the entrance. A round tower which was in Morrison's original plan was never built. There is a charming brick gate-house, however, with a battlemented turret over its entrance-passage.

The Llandaff title became extinct in 1841 and Thomastown Castle passed to cousins in France after the death of the last Earl's sister. The Comte de Jarnac

The Earls of Llandaff's castle engulfed a seventeenth-century brick mansion. Right, *the once-handsome chimney-piece in the crumbling hall, designed by Richard Morrison*

entertained large house-parties in the castle, but after his death in 1872 it remained uninhabited and began to fall into decay. In 1938 Archbishop David Mathew, a descendant of the first George Mathew and kinsman of Father Theobald Mathew, the nineteenth-century temperance leader, purchased the extraordinary ivy-clad shell with twenty acres including the walled gardens. This was done to rescue the place from demolition, but the contour of the ruined castle is changing nonetheless. In the 1970s parts of the fabric fell or were pulled down, one of the towers at the front collapsed and the hall was filled with debris.

Trim Castle CO. MEATH

The first fortifications at Trim, on rising ground above the banks of the River Boyne, were erected as early as 1172 when Hugh de Lacy built a motte and a timber tower. This was destroyed deliberately in the following year, before the castle had to be abandoned to the Irish who were attacking it. It is not clear whether the subsequent rebuilding by the Anglo-Normans was another timber tower only, or whether they began a more durable and defensible edifice in stone. The design of the surviving castle suggests that it dates from the last decades of the twelfth century, though it may have been built later in a style already antiquated. Documentary evidence suggests that the building was erected between 1210 and 1220. If the foundations were laid in the 1180s or 1190s and then completed on the same plan later it would reconcile the appearance with the evidence. When King John came to Trim in 1210 he dated his writs from a near-by meadow, which suggests that the buildings at Trim were not large enough to accommodate his court. In 1212 a payment was made for pulling down 'the tower', presumably a timber structure. In 1220 the Annals mention a castle built at Trim.

The castle on the River Boyne is the largest military construction of the Normans in Ireland. Right, *the outer fortifications*

The castle's massive, square keep has walls 11 feet thick. It differed from the usual rectangular tower of the period in having a smaller square tower projecting from each of its four faces. Three of these smaller towers survive. Their purpose is obscure. Their walls are much thinner than those of the central tower, and because of the additional angles they create and the consequent increased vulnerability, they detract from rather than enhance the defensible strength of the

202

castle. The arrangement, which was also used at Castle Rushen in the Isle of Man, can only be explained as a provision for extra chambers. At Trim there was a chapel on the second floor in the eastern tower. The entrance to the castle was situated beneath it, on the first floor. The central tower is divided in two by a cross-wall.

The castle stands in a very large bailey, over three acres in area, surrounded by a curtain wall with D-shaped turrets along one of its lengths and at three of its angles. There are two entrances to the bailey, both protected by barbicans with narrow passages. The barbican of the south gate-house contained a draw-bridge and spanned the moat. In 1399 Henry V, as Prince Hal, was lodged in this building. The D-shaped turrets and the cylindrical tower of the south gate-house indicate that the outer defences were built after the keep, possibly in the 1230s or 1240s.

Tullira Castle CO. GALWAY

Far right, *the medieval tower-house and adjoining nineteenth-century mansion where Edward Martyn received W. B. Yeats, J. M. Synge, Oliver St John Gogarty and Lady Gregory.* Above, *a stained-glass window, and* above right, *Edward Martyn's study*

The tower-house at Tullira near Ardrahan was one of several in the barony of Kiltartan which belonged in the sixteenth century to the Clanrickarde Burkes. It was acquired by a member of the Martyn (or Martin) family, one of the tribes of Galway, shortly before 1598, and has remained in the possession of his descendants to the present. Although the Martyn family remained Catholic, they were able to retain their estates and pass them on by primogeniture thanks to a special relief granted to Oliver Martyn in 1710 (*see* Dungory).

Edward Joseph Martyn (1859–1923), who inherited the family estate when an infant only fourteen months of age, was a gifted and fascinating figure of the Celtic literary and artistic revival. Playwright, author, poet, antiquarian, aesthete, art-collector, bibliophile, patron of the arts, he was the esteemed friend and associate of Lady Gregory (who was his neighbour), and of W. B. Yeats, George Moore, Oliver St John Gogarty and their circle. Yeats was a guest of Edward Martyn at Tullira in 1896, when he visited the Aran

Islands and paid his first visit to Lady Gregory at Coole Park.

Martyn was influenced at an early age by the decorative art of William Morris. As soon as he reached his majority he set about building a Revival mansion attached to the medieval tower-house, demolishing the eighteenth-century house in which the family had lived on the demesne. His building, finished in 1882, is mock-Tudor. Martyn never completely furnished it, preferring to live ascetically in the medieval atmosphere of the chambers in the old tower. These he had panelled, and furnished with simple medieval-style furniture. Some of the windows were fitted with stained glass. The 1880s were boom years in Catholic church-building, and scarcely a new church could not boast some imported stained glass, of which Mayer and Co. of Munich were the principal purveyors. Edward Martyn's energetic and enthusiastic exertions to remedy this lack of local supply resulted in the birth of a flourishing stained-glass production in Ireland, and eventually in the foundation in 1903 of Sarah Purser's famous studio for ecclesiastical art, *An Tur Gloine* (the Tower of Glass), in which Wilhelmina Margaret Geddes, Michael Healy, Ethel M. Rhind, Evie Hone and many other fine artists were to work.

Edward Martyn disposed of his extensive estates to the tenants under the Land Purchases Act, retaining Tullira with one thousand acres of well-wooded demesne and the castle of Dungory. After he and his only brother had both died unmarried, Tullira passed to the Hemphill family through the marriage of the Martyn heiress, Edward's cousin Mary, to the third Baron Hemphill. The present owner who lives there is their grandson, the fifth Baron Hemphill.

———————————

(Overleaf) *Castle Carra, Co. Mayo. Lough Carra seen through the breached wall*

Acknowledgments

We wish to thank the Irish Tourist Board, Bord Failte Eireann, without whose generous help it would not have been possible to produce this book as it is; also for their advice and offer of help, and for the illustration on p. 115, the Tourist Board of Northern Ireland. We also wish to express our appreciation to Miss Rosemary ffolliott, the Hon. Desmond Guinness, the Countess of Leitrim, Percy Paley, Esq. and Mr Brian G. F. Molloy for hospitality and to Miss ffolliott, Mr Gordon Ledbetter and the Hon. Guy Strutt for practical assistance.

We are most grateful to the owners of the many privately occupied houses who were most gracious in allowing us to visit and photograph their residences. In all cases we met with the utmost co-operation and kindness. The Directors of the Ashford Castle Hotel, the Shannon Development Co, and the monks of Glenstal were also most courteous in this respect.

Index of castles by counties